John Bunyan

by

Sandy Dengler

MOODY PRESS

CHICAGO

© 1986 by
THE MOODY BIBLE INSTITUTE
OF CHICAGO

Library of Congress Cataloging-in-Publication Data

Dengler, Sandy.
   John Bunyan.

   Summary: Follows the life of the seventeenth-century English preacher, writer, and servant of God, describing his spiritual growth, defense of religious dissent, and years spent in prison writing "Pilgrim's Progress" and other books.

   1. Bunyan, John, 1628-1688—Biography—Juvenile literature. 2. Authors, English—Early modern, 1500-1700—Biography—Juvenile literature. 3. Puritans—England—Biography—Juvenile literature. [1. Bunyan, John, 1628-1688. 2. Clergy. 3. Authors English]
I. Title.

PR3331.D46 1986   828'.407 [B]   [92]   86-878
ISBN 0-8024-4352-4 (pbk.)

4 5 6 7 8 9 Printing/LC/Year 94 93 92 91 90 89

Printed in the United States of America

Contents

Introduction

"So, John Bunyan. You're a tinker. You have a calling. Follow it."

"I have two callings, sir, tinkering and preaching, and I follow both."

"You're ignorant, and not a fit preacher."

"God chose the foolish to confound the wise."

"No one listens to you except ignorant and foolish people."

"Then, ignorant and fool, the greater they need to be taught."

"Did you come to the parish church to hear divine service?"

"No, I did not."

"Why?"

"I don't find it commanded in the Word of God."

"We are commanded to pray!"

"But not by the common prayer book."

"How then?"

"With the Spirit."

Justice Kelynge's eyes burned. "I find you guilty of preaching abroad, and not in the state church. You've already been in jail seven weeks. I send you back to prison for three months more. At three month's end, if you don't submit to go to church—the state's official church—and leave off your preaching, you must be banished from the realm. Gone from England forever. And if you are found in England after that, you will hang by the neck. I tell you plainly, John Bunyan. Away with him, jailer!"

Free men today are used to going to any church they choose—or even being able to start a new one! It is a freedom other men won for us, for once upon a time everyone had to go to one particular church or else suffer for it. For the privilege of worshiping the way he wanted to, John Bunyan suffered twelve years in prison and much other persecution.

And yet, inside the cold gray prison walls, "ignorant" John Bunyan wrote *Pilgrim's Progress*, a classic story that has been told and retold, printed and reprinted for more than three hundred years. *Pilgrim's Progress* appears in every major language of the world, telling people about God's greatest gift.

And John Bunyan himself shines as one of God's great lights in this world. This is the story of how he grew.

1

A Death in Elstow

Spring 1644

"Come on, slow-feet! Catch up!" John Bunyan leaned forward more, for his leather shoes kept slipping downhill. The dew-sprinkled grass twinkled everywhere except where his huge feet had crushed its liquid jewels. The big sack of flour on John's back chafed against his shoulder blades. He should have left his burden at the bottom of the hill. A stitch in his side forced him to stop climbing a moment. He looked downhill behind him.

Here came his sister Margaret, puffing and panting much harder than he. She was less than two years younger than he, yet she was so much smaller. John, fifteen-and-a-half, was near the end of his growing (good thing, too! Already he was the biggest fifteen-year-old around). Would Margaret ever get any bigger than she was now? More to the point, would she ever get any faster?

She clawed laboriously up the hill, climbing

with hands as well as feet. She stretched a frail, wet hand out to him. "Don't just stand there like John Fenne's ox. Help me!"

Laughing, John grabbed her wrist. With a mighty heave he dragged her the last few feet to the hillcrest. He stood now on top of the world, drawing in long, cool breaths. The dank spring breeze dried the sweat on his face and made him almost chilly. He pushed his sandy-brown hair out of his eyes with both hands.

Ah, what a glorious view! This added new meaning to the phrase "end of the earth," for even atop this high hill John could not see the ends of anything. Hill upon hazy hill stretched forever in all directions.

"We're here. Now what?" Margaret turned slowly, looking.

"See?" There's the steeple of St. Cuthbert's; that's Bedford. Elstow's right down there, of course, only we can't see our house from here. And London's off that way." He waved his arm to the south.

"Can you see London?"

"Thomas told me you can see the steeple of St. Paul's from here, but I never saw it. London's fifty miles away."

"John, do you suppose the world's really round? I can't imagine that."

John shrugged. "Looks flat to me. But then, people who travel to the New World say it is. They ought to know. No monsters out on the edge of the ocean or anything. And Sir Francis Drake sailed clear around it, he says."

"Hm. Well." Margaret rubbed her hands. "England is all quite lovely, but this isn't getting the beans planted. I'm starting back down."

John shifted the flour sack and took one last look around. For a moment he was at one with his hill and the land flowing out beyond it all squared off and dimpled by woods and hedgerows. Starting with William Bunion, his family had lived in this Bedfordshire area for four hundred years. Why, that's at least ten lifetimes!

John's grandfather Thomas had lived here his whole life until his death three years ago. John's father, Thomas, and his mother, Margaret Bentley, like John himself had been born and raised among these undulating hills. Everything this country was—strong and robust, solid farm-rich —was John as well.

"Better come!" From halfway down the hill, Margaret called a final warning. "You can't go to the fair until the beans are planted!"

The fair! With a mighty shrug, John hitched his load higher on his shoulders and bolted down the wet and slippery slope. He beat Margaret to the bottom and fell only twice doing it.

The fair! Every year, May 2 to May 5, the fair came to Elstow green. Jongleurs from far places juggled leather balls, painted bats, phony wooden fishes, and real knives. Gamesters set up little tables and invited local boys to guess which nutshell hid the dried pea. Puppeteers hunched down behind grimy curtains and let their marionettes ridicule King Charles with his haughty, spendthrift ways. Minstrels strolled through the crowds playing lutes or pipes.

The fair! Puritan preachers marched back and

forth across the green promising hellfire upon all these worldly vanities. And the things you could buy! Sweetmeats, dried fruit, smoked meat strips, pennywhistles, pins, fishhooks—John loved games and music any old time. He loved the fair especially.

By midafternoon, the beans safely tucked into their garden seedbeds, John and Margaret hurried up from the dell called Bunyan's End and headed for Elstow green. The road was not nearly as muddy as it had been a month ago, but John knew it ought to be nearly dried out by now. Wet spring. As usual, the sky was overcast, but John saw no thick, murky clouds that would promise rain. He didn't mind rain most times, but not for the fair!

Rows of tents, some in bright stripes and some with plain canvas, huddled shoulder to shoulder along the green. Most of Elstow, it seemed, strolled among the tents. In fact, half of Bedford looked to be here also. Bedford, a few miles up the road, boasted nearly a thousand people, three times the population of Elstow village. It pleased John that the Bedford folk should like Elstow fair best.

Margaret pressed against her burly brother as all these people jostled about. John wrapped a protective arm around his frail sister's shoulders. He felt very fatherly and grown-up.

"You, lad!" A skinny hand snaked out and snatched John's free arm. It jerked him and Margaret around to face a very loud salesman. "You can read, aye?"

"Aye." John couldn't read very well, but he was

proud of the fact that he could get by. "My favorites are stories about knights and dragons."

"Myths! Falsehoods! Bah! You need a Bible, lad, God's Word. And you're in luck. Today you can obtain one for five shillings. Five shillings is all it takes."

"I haven't a shilling to spare for that. G'day sir."

The bony hand stayed, clamped tight. "Ah, y're a braw lad! For you, three shillings sixpence. Geneva Bible—imported, you see, and therefore very valuable. What say ye?"

"What say I?" John thought a moment, digging into one of the unused corners of his memory. "I say you're a cheat. The Geneva Bible isn't imported at all. It's English, and it isn't worth sixpence, let alone two shillings. Not when you match it against the new Authorized Version.* And now I say also that you'd better let go of me, or I'll pluck that giant Adam's apple of yours and make applesauce."

"Me? A cheat? You cheeky bumpkin!" Usually, men no bigger than John backed off quickly when he threatened and fumed. Not this pesky fellow. "Your disrespectful tongue proves you need the Scriptures, lad. Two shillings; my final offer; and I insist you buy." He wagged a Bible in John's face.

Now John's father, a tinker by trade, knew enough heavy swearwords to outweigh his anvil.

---

*The version we call the King James. It was published seventeen years before John was born.

Thomas used them frequently, too. But John, even at fifteen, could outswear his father any day of the week. From his long vocabulary now he picked some choice curses, added an extra foul word or two, and let fly.

The salesman's watery eyes bulged wide. Those bony fingers released John's arm; the thin frame shrank and stepped back two quick strides.

John pressed his arm against Margaret's shoulders and led her off through the smelly, milling crowd. He chuckled, well pleased with himself.

Margaret sighed. "I don't know whether to burst out laughing—the look on that man's face!—or kick your shins. I hate it when you swear so fearfully, John. You know what the preachers say about swearing, and I think they're right. And by the way; where did you learn all that stuff about the Geneva Bible? You haven't been inside a church in ages, except to ring the bell."

"A mechanick preacher—you know, one of those door-to-door tradesmen who preach the Bible on the side—was at Sutton's talking about it a couple days ago." John gave Margaret a cheerful squeeze. "Wish you wouldn't worry about my tongue. Swearing comes as natural to me as breathing. If breathing isn't bad, swearing can't be all that terrible."

She snorted. "You surely didn't hear from the mechanick preachers that swearing is harmless. Those traveling preachers are almost all dissenters—Puritans or Quakers or somesuch—and they know the Scripture. They certainly don't hold with swearing."

John shrugged. He was trying to think up some lively comeback when he stopped dead in his tracks to listen. The deep-voiced bell at the church was ringing. Tolling. Margaret's blue eyes met his.

"Who died?" she whispered.

John counted the first strokes and grimaced. "A girl or woman."

Everyone else at the fair had stopped, too. People stood silently in little knots, counting the slow deep bongs. Each sad bong marked a year in the dead person's life. The toll passed two; it wasn't a baby. The toll passed six; it wasn't a child.

John was a bell ringer at the church, and he loved the job. The bell ringer did not actually have to attend church. His only job, and fun it was, was to pull on the rope. John delighted in the wild and happy bell noise of a wedding. He enjoyed drawing steadily on the rope to call worshipers on dewy Sunday mornings. But he dreaded these times, when the bell ringer must announce to the world the news of a death.

The bell ceased. For a full minute, stark silence hung over Elstow green.

"Fifteen strokes," Margaret murmured. Her eyes glistened. "John? Mary Beth is fifteen, and she's been sick. Too sick to come to the fair. It can't be her, can it?"

"Sick with what?"

"I don't know. Something that's going around. You start with chills and fever and its gets worse and—oh, John! Not Mary Beth! It must be someone else. Someone we don't know." Her voice trembled. "I'm frightened, Johnny. Only fifteen. I'm thirteen, you know."

John gathered his fragile little sister in close. He felt very fatherly just now. He also felt sad, for he had no words of comfort for her. Their father was a tinker, a man who walked from house to house, from town to town, mending things like pots and pans and harness. John and Margaret sometimes went along on these casual little journeys around the shire. No, the bell did not ring for someone they did not know, because on their travels they met everybody. Probably it was Mary Beth. If not, it was some other fifteen-year-old girl cut down untimely, and Margaret surely knew her. Oh, yes, they knew her.

John pressed Margaret's head against his broad, burly shoulder. "Don't be frightened, Little Daisy. We Bunyans are strong, and we have enough land with our cottage that we can make do. People used to get weak and sickly when food was so scarce, but times will be better now. You'll do just fine. We all will."

He released her and scooped up her small, cool hand. "And now we're at the fair. One smiles at the fair, right? That's better! Here we go!" He attached a smile to the outside of his face, but though he could put on a cheery front, the inside was not smiling. The magic of the fair had disappeared. The fun had fled. Long after it stopped pealing in his ears, the deep sad bell still tolled inside his heart.

The fair ended the night of May 5. Within a day, the salesmen and hucksters had struck their tents.

Where did they travel to next? Other fairs in other shires? The jongleurs, puppeteers, and minstrels moved on upcountry, following the spring warmth northward. The gamesters ate their dried peas, perhaps, or planted them, or invited boys in some other town to play their guessing game. The green, its grass all matted and muddy, returned to peace and quiet.

By the end of May it was clear that this year 1644 would be another lean one. In this unseasonably cold, wet weather, the seeds rotted before they could sprout. The sheep trimmed their sparse pastures so close that the grass was too short for cows to eat. The cows grew thin and bore dead calves. John had heard that in some districts last year, hungry peasants had waylaid the lumbering ox carts filled with produce for the cities. This year it would likely be the same.

In June, John's mother caught whatever it was that was going around. She was sick, miserably sick, for only a few days. Suddenly, before John could figure out exactly what death is, she died. The church bells notified the shire and rang off the years of her life one by one.

By July, Margaret, too, was sick. Numb and helpless, John sat beside her and watched the fire in her blue eyes fade, then flicker out. He still did not understand what death is and could only stand by while the church sexton came to take her body away. The heartless bells tolled thirteen for her.

In August, with John's mother dead less than two months, Thomas Bunyan quietly brought

home a brand new bride half his age.
  The bells mentioned nothing about it.

2

The Press Gang in Bunyan's End

Autumn 1644

Another chicken had died. John found it at the far end of the pasture near the old oak tree, a bedraggled pile of wet feathers. He added it to his burden of firewood and brought it along back to the house. He would hang and bleed it, but his stepmother could pluck it. That's what mothers are for, isn't it?

He tied the chicken's thin, scratchy feet together with a bit of hemp and hung it from the hook by the shed door. He could tell just by hefting it that the chicken, like all their other chickens, was scrawny and ill-fed; "all beak and bones," his mother would say. Here was why it died: one of last autumn's acorns was lodged in its throat.

The dumb bird must have been insane to try to swallow a nut so large. John whacked the head off just above the acorn and turned his back on tomorrow's supper. He crossed the muddy little yard and pushed in through the back door. He stepped instantly from the cool, dank breezes of a September evening into the warm and stuffy cottage kitchen.

Brother William, eleven years old now, sat over by the hearth, trying to whittle a spoon. Red blotches smeared his white stick; he must have cut his finger again. John drew a deep breath and coughed. A pall of smoke hung among the low beams of the ceiling. John's father hadn't fixed the ailing chimney yet.

John dumped his arm load of wood beside the hearth. The chicken that had died yesterday was bubbling away in the stew pot. John lifted the cast iron pot lid and gave the stew a stir. It smelled good, but the pot looked half empty.

He set the lid back on and plopped into the straight-backed wooden seat beside the hearth. "Another chicken dead."

William scowled. "There's arguing and fighting all over the shire. Do you suppose someone thinks we're either royalists or dissenters and they're killing our chickens?"

John shook his head. "This one died of insanity."

"A *chicken*?"

"Yeah. Really off her nut." John laughed, tickled by his pun. The smile faded. "The whole world's insane, Will. Chickens, men, everything. The hen tried to swallow an acorn bigger than her gullet. Insane. Churches squabbling with each other over who's right. Insane. The king's men are claiming they're protecting their king from dissenters, and the parliament's army claims they're protecting their king from his clergy. Insane. Our father getting married before Mama's body got cold. I walk downtown, Will, and everything looks foreign. Like they're all strangers, and yet I know them. Everything so disconnected. Maybe it's myself who's insane."

Here came John's new stepmother through the front door, an empty basket on her arm. She crossed to the hearth and dragged her shawl off her slim little shoulders. "It's getting nippy out. I certainly hope an early frost doesn't kill the beans again this year."

John mumbled something.

"Open up! Military!" Someone with a deep bass voice pounded violently on the front door.

John's stepmother gasped, wide-eyed. "Cockayne! It must be!"

"Probably." John hurried to open the door, mostly to save it from destruction.

A stout, dapper man in a military tunic charged into the middle of the room. He looked all around, glaring, as if this particular household were responsible for everything wrong in the world. A slightly built clerk followed him in and stood at his elbow, trying to shuffle a dozen sheets of paper.

"Whose household?" The clerk squinted at John.

"Bunyan, sir; Thomas Bunyan."

The wispy little man studied one sheet of paper, then another. "You're John?"

"Aye, sir."

"Not sixteen until November, according to the

church records. And a William, also. Yet a lad."

"Where's your father?" the military officer growled.

"On the road, sir. He's a tinker by trade. We don't expect him back inside the week."

"Where on the road?"

"High road toward London, sir."

"Your grandfather?"

"Died in 'forty-one, sir, three years ago. He was a chapman; he sold books and soft goods. Left me six pennies in his will, he did."

"Remarkable." The man didn't sound the least bit impressed. "We'll be expecting you to sign up come November, when you've turned sixteen. There's a brand new army in the making and a spanking new fort to live in."

"Aye, sir, Newport Pagnell. My father and I, we've watched it a-building." John nodded emphatically. Tactfully, he decided not to mention that his father shared the opinion of most of the people hereabout—that the new garrison was a huge waste of money.

"Who's in the cottage up by the ash grove?"

"Brents, sir, an older couple." Out of the corner of his eye, John saw his stepmother sit quietly on the stool near William. Why was she letting him do all the talking, as if he were the man of the house?

"November. We'll be watching for you." The officer turned smartly on his heel and marched out the door. The feeble clerk tagged along behind.

William stood open-mouthed, as if he had just watched a two-headed woman eat from both ends of a sausage. He darted to the door and slammed it shut. He turned to stare at John. "You lied to them! Father's not off toward London; he's out hear Harrowden."

"Bless you, John, lad! I was too frightened to speak." His stepmother sagged back against the wall. Her stool creaked. "If that Cockayne learned the real whereabouts of Thomas Bunyan, your father'd surely be on the army rolls tomorrow and not bringing us in a decent living. They're conscripting every male in the shire between sixteen and sixty—even some of the feeble-minded, I hear."

"You mean they might've hauled John off if he was old enough?" Will wagged his head. "Nothing he could do about it?"

"Not a thing." His stepmother sighed.

"But I heard they only conscript jailbirds into the army." William picked up his forlorn sort-of spoon and went back to whittling.

"The royalists do. Give the pot a stir, John. There's a good boy. But the parliamentary army's mostly tradesmen and craftsmen, like your father."

"I don't understand politics." William sat erect and watched John stir.

"It's easy, Will." John scouted the stew for a nice morsel to snitch before dinner. "The king's army is trying to keep King Charles in power. The official church is on his side. Then there's Oliver Cromwell on the other side; he's the leader of Parliament. He claims the king has taken over powers the Parliament ought to have, and he's got a fight going with the regular church, too. So the dissenters and Puritans are all lined up on Cromwell's side, and the church is on the king's side, and that's what they've been fighting about for years. Power and religion."

William's small hand darted in ahead of John's and snatched a bit of potato. "So whose side are you on?"

John shrugged. "Whoever gets me first, I suppose." He grabbed a chunk of hot chicken for himself and closed the pot. He flipped the meat from hand to hand rapidly, but it burned his fingers anyway.

Royalist or dissenter, dissenter or royalist? Who cared? A lot of boys John's age hid in the woods when Cockayne's press crews were out signing up soldiers. Others signed and immediately deserted. Come November, John would not go hide in the woods. There was talk that Cromwell was building a new model army, with soldiers who got paid regularly and did not have to wear their own clothes into battle. Even if army life was cold and miserable and ill-fed, as John had heard, it was better than living in this desolate house.

In an army barracks, John's grief-stricken mind would not hear Margaret's lilting laughter or his mother's crooning voice. Here, everything he looked at reminded him of his loss. There, all would be new, and memories would not plague him.

Perhaps in the army these other feelings wouldn't torment him, either. What were his feelings? He could not even sort them out. They felt something like guilt, but he had no sins to be guilty of—well, no terrible ones. They felt a little bit like hate, though John hated no one; in fact he liked 'most everybody.' They made him restless; they prickled, like chiggers. They urged him to go off and do something, but they gave him no hint as to what he might do. Was he right when he quipped that he might be going insane? Is this how people felt when they were crazy?

No. John Bunyan was big and burly and strong. Everyone in the shire agreed that he could be a friend to anybody, that he could make anyone laugh. Strong, happy people don't go crazy; only sour, weird ones do. A change of scene and a change of life would make John into a new boy—nay, into a new man.

And the best part? This was not just a power struggle between dissenter and royalist; it was a holy war. Everyone who fought in it said so. Thomas Bunyan cared nothing for things holy, and up until now, neither had John. But he could not forget the pastor's words spoken over poor Margaret's coffin. The pastor, the church vicar, had asked the Lord to admit her to heaven, but the old churchman didn't speak with much confidence. It was as if he didn't think any of the Bunyans were heaven-bound. Perhaps, just in case the vicar was right, John Bunyan ought to let some holiness rub off on him somewhere, somehow. And fighting in a holy war was as interesting a way as any to go about it.

John could hardly wait for his sixteenth birthday!

3

A Hanging at Newport Pagnell

Autumn 1646

The cold, predawn air hung heavy with the smoke of the morning fires. John Bunyan, professional soldier in the new model army, groped beneath his cot trying to find his other shoe. Everyone else in the barracks was clunking and shuffling about, too. These early roll calls were a parliamentary pain.

John had been a soldier here nearly two years now. A lot had changed in those two years. When first he had arrived in November of 1644 there were no uniforms, no real heavy guns, and too few blankets. No pay to speak of. Today John earned eight pennies daily, nearly four times what he would be making on a farm or at an anvil. He wore a uniform army tunic with the promise of more clothing items to come. It sure made identification between friend and foe easier! Discipline was much stricter now, also. John and his friends stepped over the line every now and then, but at least they knew right where the line was.

Some things, though, never change—the poor food, the endless, mindless chores, the long hours of sentry duty. John's official rank was centinel——sentry. With John Bunyan on guard, Newport Pagnell garrison was safe from stray hogs and blackbirds, the only thing John ever saw on watch. Yessirree.

Mad Thom, the only man in the barracks bigger and burlier than John Bunyan, crammed John's leather helmet on his head and gave him a shove. "You're gonna be late, my lad, and this is one party we want to be on time for."

John jogged out the door a scant pace behind Thom. "Since when do we want to be on time for a dawn muster?"

"This one's special, I hear—an execution."

"Can't be!" John hurried to his place in his column. He dropped his voice to a whisper. "No civilians on the grounds that I know of, and no one'll execute a soldier. We're too hard to get."

Thom gave him a quick, nervous "we'll see" sort of smile and stiffened, eyes front. Every soldier in the fort, nearly a thousand of them, was lined up now in blocks of tidy rows. John was surrounded by tradesmen and craftsmen like his father—brewers, cobblers, candlemakers, tanners, goldsmiths, and even a few tinkers. Someday, if the army ever got tired of him, John would take up his father's trade of tinkering. John was only eighteen, and yet he had enough money saved that he could buy his own portable anvil, and—

The unit commander shattered John's day-dreaming with a sharp order. Here came the garrison commander himself, a rollicking Irishman much after John's own heart. Commander D'Oyly strode right past the little block of wood he usually stood upon to address his troops. Instead he crossed the compound to the gallows near the stone powder magazine. Thom must be right about the hanging!

Commander D'Oyly stomped up the steps of the wooden gallows platform and turned to face his columns of soldiers. The noose dangled close to his ear. He looked about a moment at the utter silence. "Every man of you knows full well he's engaged in a holy war. Those of you who have been studying the catechism issued to you know that our goal is to free the king of enemies in high places—in the church itself." He paused. "I trust each of you is reading his catechism. I trust, too, you are all reading the Bibles issued to you."

John felt like squirming. No, he was not memorizing his catechism nor was he reading the little bound Scripture portion each soldier received. He knew it contained selections from the Bible as well as standing orders to pray before battle and to give any glory to God. That's all he cared to know.

The commander was continuing; he recited the army rules and regulations. "—Nor may you wreck a church without express permission. You know you may expect a death penalty if you run away in the heat of battle, throw down your weapons and refuse to fight, or show contempt for authority. You know that any man found drunk shall be fined a week's pay. And any man found drunk on his watch shall be hanged." He turned to a little sergeant beside him. "Bring forth the prisoner."

John swallowed hard and whispered, "I know that lad! He's from Bedford."

Flanked by guards with muskets, a luckless young soldier plodded up the gallows steps. John had seen the fellow often. In fact, just last week he had been part of the boy's unit on a sortie northward. He was a good lad, a happy chum, a man to be trusted during the heat of battle. Sure the boy drank, but that didn't make him any less a fine fellow. Lots of men drank.

The Irish accent filled the silent compound. "Two nights ago this man was found drunk on his watch, so impaired he could not have done his duty. He has been fairly tried and found guilty as charged. The penalty is death by hanging." Commander D'Oyly stepped forward a pace. "Let no man here think he is so valuable to the parliamentary army that he stands above the rules. Unholy behavior does not make a holy warrior. As Saint Peter reminds us, 'Be sober, be vigilant; because your adversary the devil, as a roaring lion, walketh about seeking whom he may devour.' Take heed lest you find yourselves wanting." He turned to the hangman. "You may proceed."

From over by the kitchen, the drummer boy began a low and melancholy drum roll.

John took a deep breath, then another. He had seen death before—his mother's slow death, Margaret's unexpected one, men killed in skirmishes with the royalists. But this young man was neither ill nor fighting.

The hangman adjusted the noose.

John couldn't watch. He loved life. He loved working and doing and playing games and joking and making others laugh. He loved simply being. In moments that sorry lad up there would stop being. John clamped his eyes tight shut, but he knew when it happened anyway; the drum roll ceased just as soldiers all around John sucked in their breath as one, a whispered gasp as wide as the parade ground. And then silence.

The commander dismissed them. With shuffling feet, hundreds of soldiers dispersed to their various duty stations.

John paused in his barracks doorway. He would pass up breakfast this morning. "What's your duty today, Thom?"

"Watch. Again." Thom wagged his huge head. "Good fortune that I'm not the drinking sort. I get watch a lot."

"Sure. That's why our rank is 'centinel.' A whole rank, just for soldiers who stand around staring at nothing and had better not drink. He was a centinel, that lad. Rules."

"Aye, rules." Thom picked up his cuirass, that heavy leather chest protector that was supposed to stop swords and arrows—but rarely did. " 'Tis not the drinking-on-watch rule that bothers me; I can see the wisdom in that. It's—it's rules in general. The rules killed him, John. Not the army or the hand of God. Rules. That makes rules the enemy, don't it?"

"Or it makes them the hand of God. Remember that mechanick preacher who was shoeing horses outside the gates yesterday? He was preaching out of the Bible. Romans, I think. Or Galatians. He said rules don't make us sin. The rules let us know that we *are* sinning. I didn't think about it until just now."

"Nor do I wish to think about it now." Thom stopped beside John in the doorway. "What's your duty today?"

"Sortie up near Essex. Thirty others, man and horse, and myself."

"Mm. Sortie. Lots of walking, maybe a little fighting and head-bashing. No thinking. Wanna trade places?"

John thought a moment. "Fine with me. Captain Hemming, near the flagpole. John Gibbs is with them."

"Thankee, John!" Thom rapped his knuckles on John's helmet. "I can do with thumping a few heads." He bounded out the door. As much as John, Mad Thom loved life.

John crossed the compound without looking toward the gallows. He did not let his eyes see the corpse hanging there. He checked in in Thom's stead, shouldered a musket, and stomped up the ladder to the catwalk. He walked from this end to that end, watching the brush and fence rows beyond the meadow. He paused at that end, then came walking back to this end—and out—and back—and out—

No wonder Thom didn't want this duty. On watch, a person has nothing to do except think. Thom didn't want to, but John did. If his rules theory was right, God did not like drunkenness. And God must not like swearing, either, if the army rules reflected God's attitude also.

Here in the army a single swearword cost you three pennies up to twelve pennies in fines, depending. If you swore a lot, you rode a narrow wooden horse with your legs spread out wide and your heels tied to the ends of a musket to keep them wide. What misery! Then again, the army might punish your swearing by pinching your tongue in a split clothespin or even boring a hole through it with a hot iron. So far, John's tongue was in one piece, but what if he should slip? Swearing came so easily!

John stopped suddenly in front of a four-foot-high post. "Instruct me, O gun support." He spoke gravely to the timber. "Oliver Cromwell calls this a holy war against ungodly men in high places. But those men are leaders of God's official church. Either those leaders are wrong or Cromwell is. So tell me, post: Who is the holy and who's the ungodly? Am I on the right side? And does it matter, so long as I fight and obey the rules?"

The post would not tell the answer. Posts are good at keeping secrets.

"Very well then, post, tell me this: Most of the soldiers in this army are tradesmen and zealous preachers of God's Word. They aren't trained by schools or churches, but they're all sure they're right. I'm surrounded day and night by preaching and piety, post. But—"

The post waited expectantly.

"—I'm also surrounded by men who drink and

swear and carry on. So, is this army made holy by the preachers, or are the sinners making it unholy? Am I closer to making it into heaven by being here, or is this army working against my chances?"

The post stared off into space with one knot like an eye and ignored him. John gave up on the speechless timber and marched to the far end again. The more he thought about all this, the more confused he got. What can a village boy know that church officials and royalty itself do not know?

"Aha! That's it!" John marched back to the post. "I'm not being paid to think. I'm being paid to be a soldier and keep watch. Let others think and take responsibility. Fighting in a holy war——declared holy by men much smarter than I, I might add—makes me holy because I'm part of a magnificent holy effort, regardless of the side I'm on."

The post looked as confused as John had been a minute ago.

"Don't you see, you woodenhead? The poor lad on the gallows was holy because he's in the holy war, too. He doesn't have to be condemned to hell just because he was drunk. I can go on swearing and Mad Thom can go on thumping heads, all in the service of Cromwell. We're doing God's work; let Cromwell take the blame if it's not what God approves of, aye?"

If silence is agreement, the post agreed. John completed his watch with a far lighter heart than when he began it.

At dusk John asked permission to go down into the hamlet half a mile from the garrison. He carefully avoided the local pub, lest he be assigned watch again tomorrow. Instead he went to Mary's cottage on the high road.

He didn't know Mary's last name; in fact, he was not certain that Mary was her first name. What he did know was that her sausages were the tastiest in Bedfordshire, and she sold them for only a few pennies. He purchased four from her and accepted a cup of tea as she fried them up for him.

They talked about Mad Thom and about the hard winter coming on. When the sausages were ready John took his leave and hurried back to Newport Pagnell, for Mary (or whatever her name was) was being courted by Thom, not he.

Mad Thom talked of marrying Mary after his army service, and settling down. Smart idea! Not only was Mary a cheerful and bubbling girl; not only did she adhere devoutly to her father's Christian faith; she was a splendid cook. What more could a man want?

When the rooster competed with the drummer to awaken camp next morning, Mad Thom had not returned. John ate a big breakfast. He forced himself to glance at the gallows on his way across the compound. The body was gone. John remembered a passage somewhere in Scripture about not allowing a body to hang on a tree past sunset. He resumed his watch—Mad Thom's watch—and found himself bored.

John Bunyan had done all his thinking yesterday. He had declared himself as holy as most men and holier than many, because he was a member of a holy army. Now he began to regret trading places with Mad Thom. Thom was getting all the action and any fun the sortie might provide. John stood around and watched nothing.

Late that day Captain Henning's patrol came straggling in. John tried to pick out Thom, but all the tunics looked alike. If Thom was as droopy as the rest of these soldiers, he would fall asleep and miss dinner. That meant they'd have to go down to Mary's tonight for more sausages. Mad Thom sure knew how to get through life with style!

John completed his watch, turned in his musket, and jogged over to his barracks. He burst in the door and slammed it loudly.

"Hah! You're back!" he roared.

But Thom was not back. His lumpy rush mattress lay forsaken beside John's.

John frowned. "John Gibbs? There you are. Where's Thom?"

John Gibbs the cooper's son, all stretched out on his own mattress, lurched himself to sitting. "Ah, John. I've been searching the will of God all the way home from our sortie. I've decided that God has important plans for you. Whatever His plan, or why He should choose a swearing man like yourself, I ken not. But then, of course, He chose the prophet Isaiah and the fisherman Saint Peter, both men of unclean lips. And Saint Paul He chose, a man party to the murder of Christians. Mysterious, His ways. And He's chosen you."

Impatiently, John dropped to one knee beside John Gibb's mattress. "I appreciate your strong interest in religion, Cooper, but let's explore God's will some other day, aye? For now I wish only a simple answer: Where's Thom?"

"He went in your stead."

"Aye, and had I gone I would now be stretched out and sound asleep, as you yourself were just now. But he's not, as you see, and—"

"He's asleep, tinker." John Gibbs interrupted gently. "In your stead. Don't you see, John? God has chosen you out for special things."

"No, I don't see." John was getting exasperated. He didn't want to hear about religion, and the cooper's words frightened him. If God chose John Bunyan for some special purpose, God was saddling John with a responsibility he did not want. John wanted no burdens on his back placed there by God or anyone else.

John Gibbs looked at him with sad eyes. "We were two miles from our destination when royalist troops set upon us. A surprise attack. Three of our members—the three leaders column right—were killed in the attack. Thom was among them. God sacrificed His Son Jesus Christ to save your soul. And as nearly as I can see, He sacrificed your friend to save your body."

4

Sausages down the Lane

1647 through 1650

The bold knight, protected head to foot in gleaming armor, rides his massive war-horse out the fortress gate. His lady waves a handkerchief "good-bye" from the ramparts, and his loyal army follows behind. Pennants and banners flutter, brilliant ribbons of color, on the warm breeze.

Soon the knight, as his army cowers in fear, will slay a hideous dragon. What a splendid feat! for it takes half his army to drag the monstrous carcass back to the fortress and the waiting lady. Ah, the glory of it all!

John snickered to himself and took two steps forward. The line in which he stood stopped again. Knights in armor? Dragons? Ladies? Solid fortress? That was another time and day; it certainly was not Newport Pagnell. Besides, knights always rode forth on clear sunny days. John stood in dark drizzle. There is no glory in misting rain.

He yearned for those mythical days, with heroes

and good, solid fortresses and dragons you could really get a sword into. Wrong and right were black and white then. These present days were much too murky. Too many so-called "experts" on right and wrong disagreed among themselves.

Even the solid fortress was doomed. Newport Pagnell garrison, built less than five years before at great cost, had been condemned by a stroke of a pen. She was not falling to some vicious enemy. No horrible act of God like fire or flood was bringing her down. Last August, Parliament had simply voted to demolish the costly fort, and that was that. Within months she would be abandoned. There is no glory in being voted out of existence by Parliament.

John took another step forward and now was first in line. "John Bunyan," he told the paymaster.

"Bunyan," the fellow mumbled. "Bun—B-U-N-I-O-N?"

"Close enough. Aye."

The man nodded and struck a squiggly little line in his record book. "You're a civilian again, John Bunyan. Go in peace, and God bless you." He slipped a paper into an envelope and handed it to John.

John thanked him, turned, and walked across the dusty parade ground for the final time. He stopped in the gate and looked back once. Then it was gone. He followed the familiar road toward Elstow. His life as a soldier was over, and he was only nineteen years old.

The future lay ahead. What lay immediately

ahead, though, were more of Mary's good sausages. John turned aside, down the lane, and knocked at Mary's door.

She answered his knock with a pretty face all smiles. "Why, John Bunyan! Do come in! Here for sausages again?"

"Aye," he grinned. "You're looking at a private citizen. I was mustered out of the army less than an hour ago."

"Now what?" She swung a pot in over her fireplace fire.

John shrugged and flopped onto the settle, that high-backed wooden seat beside the fire. "Brush up on the tinkering my father taught me. Make myself an anvil. My apprenticeship is up next year."

"Apprenticed under your father?"

"Aye, and a —" John bit his lip. He must not swear in the presence of this lovely girl, for she was every bit as religious as her father had been. Besides she was too nice a lady to hear that kind of talk. "My father's a fine tinker."

"And get married?"

"With a flock of little ones around the table. A year ago I would've cried out, 'Oh, no! Not me!' but today that's what I want. Guess I'm getting old."

"Not getting old. Growing up." She poked the sizzling sausages with a knife point. One of them made a spluttery little pop.

John laughed. "Hope I don't grow much more. Everyone complains about how oversized I am already."

She turned to stand in front of him. "You know what I mean. Picked the girl out yet?"

"I've only been out of the army an hour. Give me time."

She giggled. The smile on her face faded into a thoughtful gaze. Her face did whatever her memory thought about. She reminded him, in a way, of his long-dead sister Margaret.

He returned her gaze. "You're thinking about Mad Thom."

"No. Well, maybe, sort of. Mad Thom and his friends." She broke her gaze and returned to the sausages. "I heard you were going to Ireland."

"Wanted to. You know how much I like Captain O'Hara. He was taking volunteers to help out in Ireland, so I signed right up. Me and seventy-nine others. They gave us a month's pay in advance—"

"How much?"

"A pound sterling. We got as far as Chester, and they turned us around and marched us back here and mustered us out. Guess they don't need us in Ireland."

"Clear to Chester and you never went the short way on to Liverpool?"

"That close and never saw the ocean. Or a real ship."

She speared his sausages and popped them onto a plate. "You must be terribly disappointed. I'd love to see a ship." She handed him his plate.

He picked up a sausage and set it instantly down. He'd wait a few minutes before eating these —until the juices quit bubbling. "I'd like to see a ship, maybe, but I'm just as happy I'm not sailing on one to Ireland. I like this country right around here. Never want to go to any distant shores and alien lands. Love to see the king's ship, though. Coo, what a sight!"

"Aye, that one—that *Sovereign of the Seas*. I hear there's more gold and gilded carving and velvet and brocade on that ship than in the whole palace of the king of France." Her dark eyes danced. "Well worth a look."

"Aye." John loved watching her face in its million moods. When someday he married, he hoped he would find a girl as pretty as this one.

"With all that money poured into an old ship, can you imagine what King Charles could afford for his daughter's dowry?" Her eyes grew bigger. She reached for the teapot.

The sausages looked cool enough. John popped a piece in his mouth and burned the roof of his mouth only a little bit. "When you marry the prince of Orange you don't really need a dowry. That 'Princess' title in front of your name is dowry enough." John accepted a cup of tea to go with his sausages. "I've a sum of money saved, you know—enough to set myself up as a tinker. I don't need to marry a girl with a dowry."

"Oh. That's good." Her eyes sparkled. She seemed suddenly embarrassed. John could not see that she had said anything embarrassing. She must have been thinking it. She sat on the hearth at his feet. "I've a dowry, you know, that's worth far more than gold."

"Really?" He started on his second sausage.

"Two books. *The Plain Man's Pathway to Heav-*

en, by John Dent, and *The Practice of Piety*, by
Lewis Bayly. Why, my father practically memo-
rized the both of them. He said my husband
should have them, because I deserve nothing less
than the best possible servant of God."

Two religious books seemed a pitifully dull
dowry to John, but he said nothing. On the other
hand, a girl could bring a far worse dowry to a
marriage.

John took his leave two hours later, a little reluctantly, for he liked to be around this bright,
warm girl. He hurried down the road toward Elstow and Bunyan's End. He could still reach home
by dark if he kept moving. Fortified by Mary's delicious sausages he strode briskly along the road.

That smoky, drizzly overcast was clearing. This
afternoon would end fair. The first streaks of evening light slipped out from under the dull gray roof
of clouds. It turned the whole countryside gold.
Sail to foreign lands? Not when your own native
country is golden!

At dusk, John Bunyan, ex-soldier, was home.
Before the year was out he would cast a portable
anvil in iron and take up his father's profession of
mending pots and pans and such. He would carry
his sixty-pound anvil, with all his tools, from
house to house around the shire.

That same year he would realize why Mary ap-
pealed to him so much. He would return to her
house and marry her, to bring her home to a little
cottage in Elstow. He would enjoy her good cooking and even read some in her dowry.

By January of 1649, Parliament had become

wearied of King Charles and his wild spending. As the official church howled and the dissenters cheered, Parliament ordered the king beheaded. Oliver Cromwell became the country's leader, and he approved heartily of dissenters and mechanick preachers.

John wasn't surprised that suddenly all he heard, all around him, was the preaching of tradesmen and laborers; that was what Cromwell's army had been made of. John regretted that his king was dead, but religion and politics didn't interest him. Well, maybe religion was starting to, a little. It was those books of Mary's—

In early 1650 John became father of a baby girl, and they named her Mary. Only one dark cloud dulled his bright and happy new life as a tinker and husband and father:

Little baby Mary was born blind.

5

The Game on Elstow Green

Early 1650s

John Bunyan squirmed uncomfortably on the hard wooden church pew. He glanced over at Mary, with blind Mary and baby Elizabeth sitting between. Mary looked smug. Composed. Quite happy with the sermon. She would. She agreed with everything Pastor Christopher Hall was saying.

The pastor of Elstow church stabbed toward the ceiling with a bony finger to emphasize his message. "The book of sports, my brothers and sisters!" He waggled a little book in the air; John knew it well. "This little book contains the rules for every vile sport and pastime. It lists all the games one might play on the Sabbath day! The Sabbath!"

John grimaced. He was planning on a little tip-cat after dinner.

"Parliament ordered this book burned eight years ago," the pastor bellowed, "but it's still around because of sinful men. Every hour wasted in play is an hour lost to prayer. Lost to Scripture study. Lost to the contemplation of God's sovereign will."

John tried in vain to find a softer spot in the pew.

And now Pastor Hall was boring into John with clear and angry eyes. Among all the sinners and possible sinners in this whole congregation, he was looking squarely at John! "Will you waste your life in idle games? Will you spend your time uselessly? Will you follow the siren song of this evil little book, or will you honor the Sabbath as it ought to be honored? Will you turn to God and mend your sporting ways?"

The pastor droned on a few more minutes. The congregation sang a closing hymn. John joined in the singing, for he loved any music, but his conscience burned. Every bit as much as John loved music, he loved sports more.

When at the close of the service he left the church with Mary and the girls, his conscious still ached.

"I hope you were listening today," Mary said quietly.

The bright sun hit John in the face as they stepped out into the street. "Aye, I was listening. You've talked me into coming to church with you. Now you look to change me into a completely different sort of man. Isn't church enough?"

"There are two purposes to church, John. One is to worship God together. The other is to hear God's Word and try to be a better person for Him."

"I'm a bell ringer. A good one, too. That's serving Him—ringing the church bells."

"It also happens to be jolly good fun for you, so you're serving yourself as well. I'm talking about giving up things *He* doesn't like."

John grunted and glanced at her. The sunshine made her rich hair fairly glow. Oh, but she was a pretty lady! He couldn't argue with such a lovely girl. He let the whole topic die. Perhaps she and the pastor were right. Perhaps it was time to give up playing games and settle down. Oh, but how he loved to play!

Mary carried Elizabeth into their little cottage on her hip, and John carried blind Mary. He loved this pleasant little house. It was right in Elstow on the bend of a street. John loved being surrounded by people. He loved the village life.

Perhaps he should split some kindling. "How long before dinner?"

"It's ready now. I prepared it before we left." Mary busied herself at the fire.

"Ah!" John plunked into his chair at the table. "Smells like lamb stew."

"Looks a lot like lamb stew, too." Mary brought him a large dish of the most marvelously fragrant, dark, rich stew. Hearty chunks of meat, potatoes, and onions peeked from a thick broth. A bay leaf poked its pointy little tip out from between two chunks.

John said grace quickly and popped into his mouth the first chunk his spoon found. Potato. He crushed it with his tongue, savoring its flavor. Aaah, potato! He scooped up another morsel. Onion. Sweet, soft, silky, slippery, rich-flavored on-

ion. Aaah, onion! He sought out a lamb chunk.
Aaaah.

He pulled the bay leaf out, licked it, and laid it
aside.

All the torture in John's conscience dissolved in
this marvelous dinner. He relished every bite. He
licked his lips. He accepted seconds. He scraped
the dish clean. He sat back. Peace. Little Mary
dozed off, and Elizabeth was asleep. Mary sat
down across from him with her cup of Sabbath
tea. She did not bother with household chores on
the Sabbath. This was her day of rest, and she appeared as much at peace as he. She smiled across
the table at him. He beamed back.

"Mary, I'm a happy man! Everything in life sat-
isfies me."

"Even hauling that heavy anvil all over the
shire?"

"I've carried heavier burdens. How about you?
Are you content?"

"Pretty much so. For myself, yes. But John, I do
wish you were a more pious man. I fear so for your
soul."

He nodded. "I admit I swear too much. And I do
enjoy a game or two on the green on a Sunday afternoon. But Mary, Sunday's the only day the other lads and I can get a game together. I'm working
and on the road all the rest of the week. You understand, don't you?"

"I understand you're not observing the Sabbath." She leaned forward. "John, I worry about
you so! You know what God thinks of all your
wrongs."

"I don't wrong my fellowman. I'm fair and honest. That must count for something."

"It's all very good, but good works don't balance out sin. Pastor Hall said that last week."

"Aye, always talking of a bright future—and a bleak present. Well, I prefer a little fun in the present as well as the future."

She pleaded another ten minutes, and John ignored what she was saying; he was finding that easier and easier to do lately. Finally he announced for himself a quiet afternoon walk and hurried outside into the bright sunshine.

Small fluffy clouds, like sheep scattered across a hillside, sprinkled the blue sky. What a fine day! Warm air stirred around his cheeks and mussed his rusty flyaway hair. Mary was right. Pastor Hall was right. He must give up his worldly games on Sundays. He might walk over to the green and watch others play, which was almost as much fun, but he himself would stay on the sidelines. Starting now he would make himself a better man, to please Mary.

The Elstow village green, that trim little pasture in the middle of town, was busy this fine day. Old men sat on the benches, leaning on their canes and nodding, half asleep. Children by the score ran up and down the lush green grass. In a few years John's children would be here, too. Their laughter rang like angel music. Three women sat barefoot in the grass, knitting. Two cows and a goat grazed contently.

And here were John's friends, all cheerful fellows. They were deep into a rousing game of tipcat, John's very favorite pastime.

It was Big Harry's turn now. The huge, hairy blacksmith stood in the center of a measured circle. He was given a battered wooden shuttle called the cat. He tossed it in the air a couple times and caught it. He hefted his great clumsy club called the cat staff. And now he threw the cat straight up high. As it dropped he swung his club. With a solid *whack* the wooden shuttle sailed high and plopped down several rods beyond the circle.

Harry grinned. "How's that, eh? There's Johnny! Join us, John.'

"Not today."

"Eh? Won't show me how it can be done better?"

Next up was Clive Perkins, the local barber-surgeon. His arms were like tree trunks, his hands as broad as dinner plates. How could a man that burly give you a close and delicate shave, let alone perform minor surgery? He gave the cat one careless flip into the air. With a mighty swing he clubbed it halfway across the green.

"That's 'ow hit's done, 'Arry," Clive boasted smugly.

Clive's boasting did it. John could hang back no longer.

"So that's the way, eh, Clive?" John took up the cat staff. Harry threw him the cat. He rubbed his fingers across the cool, dented wood. He hefted the bat, its weight so familiar to him. This was by far his best sport. He wasn't about to let Clive boast.

"Clive, you might get started up the road

towards Bedford, if you intent to catch."

Harry roared. Behind John the Rowe boy laughed.

John knew that to get the best distance you must strike the cat squarely, broadside. Instead of flipping it, he lofted it off the palm of his hand.

Whock!

The cat arched high into the fluff-studded blue sky. Every head there followed it—the first thing they'd all agreed on that day.

"That, Clive," John announced, "is how it's done."

He had earned the next play.

For a moment, as an echo, he thought he heard Mary's sweet voice: *Oh, John, please give up your worldly ways.* Nonsense! It was his imagination only.

"John!"

The voice was not one of his friends here on the green. It rumbled, deep; it had no trace of the farm-country accent; it rang with authority; it sounded dreadfully sad. And yet—

"John."

John let the cat staff drop to his side. Hastily he looked all around. The Rowe lad and Harry were looking at him strangely.

"John."

He looked up. There, in amongst the fluffy, sheep-like clouds, Jesus Himself was looking down at John and frowning sadly. How did John know who it was? He just did; that was all. Jesus. John glanced around him. Everyone was staring at him now, and no one was looking at the sky. No one but John could see this thing.

"John," said the vision, "will you leave your sins and go to heaven, or will you have your sins and go to hell?" The vision faded slowly, quietly. The sky was again as it had been before, white puffs of cloud in a blue vault.

John stared at Harry. "Did you see—?" No, Harry's face made it plain he had seen nothing. Clive hadn't seen. John wheeled around to stare at the Rowe boy. The boy stared back.

John felt as if someone had punched him. It was a vision—a dream dreamed in daytime. And yet the figure was certainly Jesus Christ. John almost tossed the cat away.

But wait! Jesus wasn't just talking about this Sunday afternoon game of tipcat. He had said "sins." *All* wrong doing. That meant all John's many, many faults. There was no way in the world that John Bunyan could shed all his sins. No one could be totally perfect. There was no hope that he could give up doing everything that was wrong and frowned-upon. Besides, even church men sinned.

Even if John abandoned this game—even if he never played tipcat again—all those other sins would doom him.

"No!" he cried out loud. "It's hopeless! I'm damned." And he did not mean it as an oath this time. He meant it as truth exactly the way he said it. He would be damned to hell whether he tried very hard or did not try at all. He could never make himself perfect. He was doomed.

And if he was doomed, he might as well enjoy to

the fullest whatever time he had in this life. Since he could not change things he would begin living life to the fullest. Right now!

He lofted the cat high in the air and drove it clear off the green.

6

A New Man in Elstow

Early 1650s

The high road through Elstow village was made of the stuff every high road is made of—dirt. Centuries of use had packed it down; shoes, bare feet, animals' hooves, iron wagon tires, and wooden cartwheels all did their part. In dry weather, the top half inch of road was chewed to dusty powder. In rain, the powder turned into slippery, clinging slime. The wet goo made oxen lame by packing itself up between their cloven feet. The slop stuck to shoes, to be tracked into well-scrubbed cottages.

It was raining now, the first rain after a week-long dry spell, and the Elstow high road was just plain slurpy.

The rain didn't help John's foul mood any. For a month now, ever since that frightening vision of Jesus, he had been feeling droopy. The rain and the grasping mud added to his droop.

He was tired, too. He carried his tool pack and anvil all the way in from Houghton Conquest to-

day, and his back ached. Ah, but now he was near-
ly home. Soon he could shed this heavy burden.
Soon he would be tasting Mary's good cooking.
Soon.

Two young men, apprentices to the candlemaker, approached him laughing. John knew
them. They must have been allowed to go home
early today. What were their names? Robert and
Morgan? He couldn't remember. Here came Robert or whoever up the street whistling. Morgan or
whoever suddenly darted up behind him,
snatched his hat from his head, and ran.

With a roar, Robert took up the chase. They
came running down the road past John. As they
went by, both of them splashed through the puddle beside him. Ice-cold, muddy water sloshed all
over John's legs.

That did it! John wheeled around and yelled at
them. He turned loose a string of swearwords.

"John Bunyan!" A woman's sharp voice barked
out right behind him. He turned toward the bakery shop.

Mrs. Lowe, the baker's wife, leaned out her open
shop window and wagged a finger in his face.
"You are the ungodliest fellow for swearing that I
ever heard in all my life! For shame! For utter
shame! You'll spoil every young person in this
whole town if they come anywhere near you. I'm
not a godly woman myself, and I've heard a word
or two, but your mouth is absolutely disgraceful!"
She leaned back and slammed the shutters.

John's mouth fell open and he just stood there.
Cold water drained into his shoes. He gathered his

wits together and continued on home. He stomped in the door and let his anvil and tool box fall from his shoulders with a ringing, thunderous clang.

Mary jumped a foot and turned to him. "Here you are, obviously. Dinner is waiting."

John flopped into his chair, wearied by more than just the miles he had traveled. "You know that Mrs. Lowe, the baker's wife?"

"Aye. A loose and ungodly wretch. Screams at her husband a lot."

"That's the one! Loose and ungodly is right. You know what she had the nerve to tell me? That my swearing offended her. Her! She's never seen the inside of a church in her life. She chewed me right into the ground."

"Good!" Mary reached for the ladle.

"Good? *Good?* Somebody pious might have the right to snarl at me, but not the likes of her!"

Mary clunked his dinner down in front of him. "Wrong is wrong, regardless of who points it out to you."

John sputtered. This was not the sympathy he had expected. He picked up his spoon.

"Grace?" Mary asked pleasantly.

"Grace," he muttered and put his spoon back down. He thanked God for His generosity and picked up his spoon again. "You ate already?"

She nodded. "We didn't know when you'd be home, and the girls were hungry."

He picked at his roast chicken and broken-bread stuffing. "I had cause, you know. It was those two boys working for the candlemaker."

"Robert and Morgan?"

"Those two. Came tearing upstreet and splashed cold water all over me. It's still running into my shoes. Ice water."

"You're not made of wool, that you'd shrink. They're good boys. Full of energy, but good boys. If it's them you were swearing at, I agree with the baker's wife. Shame on you!"

John's ears burned. That baker-woman's tongue-lashing had ripped him like a sharp knife. And now here was Mary, his beloved Mary, ripping some more. The worst of it was, he knew they were right. Mary had always been right.

"Margaret," he murmured.

"What?" Mary frowned.

"My little sister Margaret. She died young. She used to get so angry with me because of my tongue. It hurt her. She said so."

"It hurts me, too."

"But I never swore at Margaret, or at you and the girls either, though my father swore at me many a time."

"I know, and I'm glad you don't. Your foul language hurts me because I know how much it hurts God. John, you can't dance through life cheerfully while you cause God so much pain. Sooner or later He's bound to lose patience with John Bunyan. And then—" She sighed.

"But how could I quit? My whole life—"

She was looking at him eye to eye, and her cheeks were wet. His bad language had reduced her to tears, and that cut even deeper than Mrs. Lowe's scolding had. "I don't know," she whispered.

Suddenly she sat up straighter. "Remember what Jesus said? 'Sufficient unto the day is the evil thereof?' Try not to swear anymore today. Just today. Let tomorrow take care of itself. And then tomorrow morning when you get up, tell yourself: 'I will not swear today. Only today.'"

He wagged his head doubtfully. "I don't know—"

"You don't get to Harrowden or Houghton Conquest in one great leap. You get there one step at a time."

"I could try it. But even if I managed to stop swearing, what good would it do? Jesus said, 'Give up your sins.' Lots of sins. If I give up swearing, there's still all those others."

"What good would it do? It would please God. Isn't that good enough? And you wouldn't be giving the children of this shire such a terrible example. They all look up to you, you know, because you love little children and they know it. You're a large man and jolly, and you play games with them. And you ring the church bells. And then these children who admire you so hear your swearing."

John thought about all the laughing little children who met him along the way, and about the Rowe boy who so obviously admired him. "I'll do it!" John cried. "I shall please God as well as any man in England could please Him. And I'll start right now—" He clamped his hand over his mouth. "Almost let one slip there."

She laughed, and her laugh tinkled and lilted. She got up suddenly and crossed to the mantel. She brought him half her dowry, the book called

The Plain Man's Pathway to Heaven. She thumbed through it and found her place. "One of the conversations in the arbor between Theologus the divine one and Asunctus the ignorant man. Theologus guesses that there are a hundred thousand swearwords used in England every day. He claims some men put in a hundred a day."

"That's me, sometimes." John sat back in his chair.

"Theologus says, 'Even little boys and children rap out oaths in a most fearful manner.' You see, John? You can poison a child's mind. And then Theologus lists some oaths: 'by my faith, by my troth, by our Lady, by Saint Mary, as God will judge me.' "

John's ears burned hotter. He had used three of those very oaths today, plus a whole lot more.

Mary continued. "Then Asunctus—that's Ignorant—says, 'How about the man who swears by a cock or mousefoot?' "

"And Theologus says, 'It's equally sinful to swear by creatures.' "

"And Ignorant says, 'What then can we swear by?' "

"Now listen to this, John. And Theologus says, 'Swear not at all.' " She turned the page. "And then they get off on the subject of lying, which, thank God, you do not do." She closed the book and started to stand up.

"Leave it here," John asked. "I'll read some in it tonight, while I'm drinking my tea."

She smiled so brightly and happily that he was sorry he had not promised more.

During the next week, and into the next month,

John absolutely surprised himself. This terrible habit of his, this swearing, this unruly tongue, had been broken. He rarely slipped at all, and when he did the oath was mild.

He was so immensely pleased with this new man, this new John Bunyan, that he decided perhaps he would work harder to improve further. Bell ringing. That was an important point. He was doing it for the church, yes. But it also gave him much pleasure. That might mean he was really doing it not for God but for himself. With a twinge of regret, he resigned his post as bell ringer.

But the urge to ring the church bells did not go away slickly, the way swearing had. Sunday mornings he found himself dawdling behind his family, listening to the bells. Sometimes, when the big bells called vespers, he would leave his warm cottage and go stand in the cold and wind-blown street, his head craned back, to see and hear, to listen.

The bells' songs filled the air, and they filled John's heart and soul as well. John loved music of all sorts, and bell music was the song closest God, it seemed. By standing in just the right spot, by a little garden gate on High Street, he could watch the bells sway back and forth in the steeple top.

And then, an ugly, persistent thought spoiled his bells. John knew how those bells were attached to the steeple. They were hung from heavy wooden yokes. The yokes were hundreds of years old. Surely their wood was checked and splitting after all those years. What if one of the bells should fall?

John could picture in his mind what would hap-

pen if, for instance, the big brass bell should fall.
With a horrible crack the yoke would split and
cave downward. Slowly, majestically, then faster
and faster, the enormously heavy bell would drop
through the belfry catwalk. It would splinter the
roof timbers under the steeple.

Like a great fist of doom it would punch
through attic and ceiling timbers. It would come
crashing down through the ceiling onto—

—the unsuspecting bell ringer!

John shuddered. The imaginary picture was so
vivid, so hideous, he could not bear to watch the
bells swing anymore. From that time on he listened to the bells from afar—and carefully avoided being near the steeple when they rang.

Bells and swearing conquered, the next step in
the new and improved John Bunyan must be cor-
rection of his dancing. The mechanick preachers
all shouted against dancing. Pastor Hall wagged
his head and repeated over and over how devilish
dancing was. Wicked.

Yes, John would definitely give up dancing.

It was such an easy decision to make.

It was such a difficult thing to actually do.

Every time John saw a set in progress, he wanted to join in. Every time the lutes and violas began to play, John felt the urge to dance. And now
and then, he did.

But do or die, he determined to rid himself of
this overpowering urge to join in dancing.

It took the new, improved John Bunyan the better part of a year.

7

Two Women on a Doorstep

Early 1650s

When you repair a clock it runs better. When you grease an axle, the wheel turns more smoothly. It would seem, were you to improve upon something, that it should be better afterward than before.

John Bunyan was improving himself in all sorts of ways, yet he was much more miserable now than he had ever been before in his life. Blue sky looked gray. The voices of his beloved bells had lost their charm. He found himself snapping angrily at Mary, often for no reason at all. He detested carrying his heavy anvil and tools all over the shire. Nothing was right. Everything was dismal. God might be as pleased with him as with any man in England, but the strain was ruining him.

He strolled down High Street in Bedford now, on his way home. He dragged his feet and slogged through the dust. He didn't want to carry this burden a foot farther. He didn't want to walk the few miles more to his front door. He didn't even want to talk to Mary. He wanted—he didn't know what he wanted. Everyone on the green today looked happier than he felt. It made his low spirits lower still.

He passed the half-timbered Moot Hall and the green. He turned down toward the River Ouse and the Swan Bridge.

Two women sat on a doorstep by the road. That was not unusual. On this fine day a lot of people were out enjoying the good weather. The women's fingers flew as they knitted bone lace. That was not unusual either. Knitting bone lace was a local industry. Nearly all the women in Bedford made lace for a little extra money. It appeared these women could use extra money, too. Their faded, patched clothes told John they were very poor. And yet, only their outside was poor. These ladies glowed with joy. They were incredibly rich inside.

They were talking as he passed. Normally he would not care what they said. John was not a gossiper. But their voices lilted. The happiness attracted him.

"Ah, without His love I'd be so wretched," the one woman was saying. "Years I spent in misery before knowing Him."

She must be talking about a lover. That did not interest John. He walked on by.

"And yet He's known and loved us since the beginning of time. That is what fascinates me so. 'Tis mystery," said the other.

"Blessing, too," added the first. "Blessing to be

safe in His love. How many people speak the name
of Jesus, and how few know His love!"

John stopped. For years he had used the name
of Jesus in swearing. *Safe in His love*. He walked
back to the two women.

"Excuse me. I overheard in passing. Safe in His
love. Love of Jesus?"

"No other love offers safety." One woman scoot-
ed over on her doorstep. "Sit awhile, lad. You look
tired with that burden. Put your pack aside.
You're the tinker John Bunyan, are you not?"

"I am, from down in Elstow."

"I'm Sister Coventon, and this is Sister Bosworth. How do!"

Sister Bosworth peeked out around her wide
friend with a happy grin. "How do!"

"The way you were speaking—" John stam-
mered a bit, searching for the right words and not
finding them. "It's as if joy were forcing you to
speak so. As if you had found a whole new world."

Mrs. Coventon smiled, and her face lit up as if
her eyes were candles. "Where were you born?"

"Harrowden, mum. Raised in Bunyan's End hard
by Elstow. My family goes back four centuries at
least."

"You must know that end of the shire pretty
well."

John grinned. "Every tree and stone. My
father's a tinker also, and I traveled with him
when I was young. I know every road and every
soul around."

"I suppose, lad, if you moved to some other

shire it would take a bit of time before you were comfortable in the new place like you are in the old."

"I should think so!" John frowned. Where was this woman leading?

"You say we sound as if we've found another world. Well, we have. Bedford here is where our bodies live. Like you, I was born here, and I know every picket and post. But Sister Bosworth and I have been born into another world as well. It's the world of God's love and mercy. We've just begun to get comfortable in that new world, and it's giving us endless joy."

John's heart ached now more than his muscles ever did. His soul yearned more than his mind ever had. "I would give anything to enter the world you talk about."

"It cannot be bought. There's nothing you can buy it with, and nothing you can do to earn it."

"Oh, but I've reformed myself. I've broken off my swearing and dancing and—"

"That's very good!" The woman's sweet voice interrupted his list. "And do you now have the world we're talking about?"

"No."

She nodded. It was exactly the same *there! you see?* nod that John's natural mother had so often made. "The way to eternal life is to call upon God first. Ask Him to forgive your sins first. Ask His mercy first."

"I'm constantly asking His mercy for something."

"And what is the mercy you ask for?"

John shrugged. "You know—uh, mercy."

"Mercy is receiving less punishment than you deserve. After He has forgiven your sins—and He will as soon as you ask Him—then when you re-form yourself, as you call it, you can do it to please Him and to say thank you for His favor. You won't be buying your way to heaven, for you can't do that anyway. You'll be expressing gratitude by doing what you know He wants of you."

John gobbled up her words the way a starving man takes in food. "I tell Him I've sinned? Even when He already knows it? And then promise not to?"

"Ask Him to give you eternal life through His Son, Jesus. Jesus is the way. God will do that. Then promise to make Jesus Lord in your life, which is exactly what you've just been saying. If Jesus is Lord, you do what pleases Him."

"That seems too easy! Don't I have to *do* something?"

Mrs. Bosworth cackled brightly. "Ah, lad, it's the easiest thing in the world, and it's the hardest! God will create a new man in you, and Satan will fight you bitterly because of it. The old man in you can create quite a stir, too."

"Ah." John laughed. "I'm used to war going on inside me. I've had some of that these last few months, believe me!"

Mrs. Coventon raised a cautionary finger. "If any of your sins have hurt another person, you must do the best you can to correct the wrong. That's called 'restitution.' "

"Aye, I see!" John leaped to his feet and

snatched up his pack. It was not nearly so heavy now as it had felt before. "I must run tell Mary! Thank you, good dames! Thank you!" He took two flying steps, skidded to a stop, and turned around. "Where do you worship, you and others of your faith?"

"We use the Bedford church building, but we meet separately from the high church services. We started meeting in sixteen fifty. We've just now elected ourselves a pastor, John Gifford. Perhaps you know him."

"I've heard, aye. He was in the royal army and an altogether sinful fellow. Then he turned clear around and became an altogether pious man. The whole shire talks of it."

"Turned around. Yes! That's exactly what 'convert' means. He's a perfect pastor for us, for he's seen both sides of the fence."

"Aye, no doubt. Thank you. G'day!" He wheeled and ran, his weariness forgotten.

As he entered Elstow the church bells began to ring. A wedding party came pouring out the church doors as he passed. The bells continued their merry song as he slammed in through the door of his little cottage. He dropped his pack with a mighty clang.

Rudely awakened from her nap, little Mary began to howl.

"John! Now look what you've done!" Mary wailed.

John wrapped his thick arms around Mary and swept her off her feet. He swung her in a happy circle. "I've found a whole new world! This Sunday let's go to church at Bedford town!"

"What? Who? Whatever. John, put me down! Bedford?"

"Not that far to walk. Three miles about. There are these two rich ladies who—well, actually, they're dirt poor—but rich! And they—" Somehow, the lovely flowers of his thoughts lost all their petals in his speech. How could he describe this wonderful new feeling? He let Mary's feet touch the floor. "I just—something happened, you see, and—"

He started again. "Remember I told you about the time I once fell out of a boat on the river?"

"And you couldn't swim."

"But the Lord preserved me. And the time I killed an adder by the roadside?"

Mary shuddered. "And broke the snake's fangs out with your fingers."

John sobered. "And Mad Thom. He took my place and never came back. God's hand saving me, Mary. And now I'm beginning to wonder if old John Gibbs wasn't right. He said God was saving me for something special. Maybe a life of service or something."

"You're trying to improve for Him. And you're doing much better."

"But that's not—" How do you explain light to someone who cannot see it? John sighed and gave his pretty wife a squeeze. " 'Tis all so confusing, Mary. Perhaps it will flatten itself out smoothly one day soon, so that I can see what God wants."

The church bells, reluctantly it seemed, quieted their merry pealing.

8

Puddle in the Road

Early 1650s

A puddle. Just a simple, ordinary puddle. Rain from an afternoon thunderstorm had collected in this rut in the road. A few bits of hay and bark floated on it. One end was greenish from horse leavings, and the other end shone golden as the late-afternoon sun slipped through the clouds.

John stopped and stooped beside the puddle to watch. A mosquito hovered above its surface. Some huge horseflies walked to its muddy edge, apparently for a drink. In the mud beside it a cloud of white butterflies settled and flittered and resettled.

John glanced skyward. This puddle would dry up in a few hours if no more rain came. No loss. Except for the butterflies, it seemed to serve only undesirable insects.

He thought about the words of Jesus: *If ye have faith as a grain of mustard seed, ye shall say unto this mountain, Remove hence unto yonder place;*

and it shall remove; and nothing will be impossible unto you. That was in Matthew someplace—seventeen twenty? Somewhere there.

If John Bunyan had real faith in God, like Jesus talked about, he could tell this mud puddle to dry up and it would. Right away. Here would be an excellent test. Did he really have faith, or was all his ripening religious interest useless? He stood up,

took a deep breath,

pointed to that puddle, and—

and—

and lost his nerve. He'd better pray first. Hadn't Jesus said something about this faith not coming except through prayer and fasting? He knelt beside a roadside hedge and asked the Lord to honor his test. He asked again for good measure. Now he stood up and squared his shoulders, and pointed to that puddle, and and lost his nerve again. What if it didn't dry up? What if his test proved that he had no faith? That he was lost forever? He could not even bear to think about it! Lost forever after all his trying.

Frightened by the chance he had nearly taken just now, he turned his back on the puddle, leaving it to dry up on its own. He snatched up his tool sack and anvil and hurried down the road home. He would not tell Mary about this. He was ashamed of his lack of courage; he feared for his lack of faith. Mary would probably understand; then again, she might not.

That night he climbed wearily into bed and listened to the rain whisper among the tree leaves

outside their cottage window. The puddle would
be there in that rut now, unbothered by faithless
men. He heard the constant *blip blip blip* as the
rainwater dripped from the roof thatch to the little ditch dug along the side of his cottage. He
could hear an occasional drip inside here, too. He
really ought to get the roof thatched again. For
two pounds six shillings he could get a cheap
grass thatch. For four pounds, the thatcher would
do his roof in sturdy reed thatch that would last a
hundred years.

The rain was gone. There sat those two poor
women of Bedford on a sunny hillside. They made
their lace and talked together about Jesus. The
hillside was bright and warm, and their conversa-
tion was just as sunny and bright and warm. Mrs.
Coventon was saying how their own righteousness
counted for nothing. And chubby Mrs. Bosworth
was bobbing her jowly head up and down eagerly,
agreeing that Christ's righteousness was what
would carry her into heaven.

Then Mrs. Coventon was explaining how Jesus
helped her resist the temptation to unrighteous-
ness.

Then snow was coming down around John's
ears. The little flakes were so cold they stung if
they touched his bare skin. Those women were enjoying summer sun, and John was stuck here in
cold winter darkness.

A great stone wall separated the warm world
from this cold one. John could see the women only
by peeking through a small hole in the wall. How

he longed to join them! He began frantically to search for any crack in this wall, any loose stones he could pry free.

Here was the smallest of breaks in the stone face. The wall had cracked, as walls do sometimes when the soft ground beneath them settles. Without a second thought, John forced his head into the crack. He jammed his shoulders in. And now he was stuck!

He pushed and squeezed, twisted and pulled. The cold stones clamped around him. He was tired. Exhausted. What if he could never get back out? How could he reach that warm sun? Finally his head eased out into the brightness. His feet still struggled in the dark wet snow. He squirmed. He fought. Now his shoulders were through. Suddenly he popped out and was walking through the whispering grass. No longer weary, he sat among the women and talked along with them as they praised their Lord. His heart sang, although he could not remember any of the words they were saying, even as they said them. The light and heat of the sun warmed him clear through.

Rainwater still dribbled in the ditch, but the wind had changed. John awoke as the rain blew against the window shutters.

A dream.

It was all a dream, that struggle to reach the warm hillside.

"John?" Mary, in bed beside him, was propped on one elbow. "You're bouncing all over the bed and muttering."

John could barely see her in the gloom. Few places are as dark as the inside of a cottage at night with the shutters closed. "You don't have to squeeze through some crack, Mary. Your father was a godly man. He led you by the hand to that warm hillside."

"Whatever are you talking about?"

"My father didn't show me any bright new world. He only taught me how to swear."

"John, wake up! Are you awake?" She shook him.

He laughed. "Yes, Mary, I'm awake. And I'm sorry I woke you. It was a dream. A wonderful dream." He lay back in the absolute darkness and stared at the ceiling timbers he could not see. "I'll do better than that for our children. I'll lead them to the hillside. Mary's talking well now."

"Constantly." Mary flopped back, too. "All day, words flowing like water down a mill race. Talk talk talk."

"I'll never teach her a word God wouldn't approve of. She'll learn clean speech. So will our other children, I promise. Mary?"

"Hm?" She sounded half asleep already.

"You do approve, don't you? To become members of John Gifford's congregation in Bedford?"

"Yes," she muttered sleepily. "Good."

"We might even think about moving to Bedford. Nearer church, then. And most of my customers are in and around Bedford now. Not so far to walk with that anvil. Wouldn't have to thatch this roof. Thatch the new cottage if it needs it."

"Mmm hmm." Mary was nearly asleep.

Was he saved for certain? His doubts wore him out. He almost wished he were a dumb animal, like a goat or a cow. Goats and cows never had to worry about having sinful natures. They didn't fear any lack of faith. Poor John Bunyan's religion was swinging back and forth like bells in a steeple.

To keep his mind from worry so he could get to sleep, John made his imagination think about bells. Beautiful bells, loud bells, gentle bells, bells swinging and singing his weary mind to sleep.

9

Wee Matthias in High Street

Spring 1656

"Why, it's wee Johnny Bunyan! Advance one more step, and I'll stuff your ears into your boot tops!" The bear-sized fellow, every bit as tall and as wide as John, stopped in the roadway, ankle deep in mud. He tossed his heavy pack aside as if it were a bundle of straw. He stood boldly, his hands on his hips. Even in this drizzling rain his hair was as red as maple leaves in autumn.

"Hah! Wee Matthias Crowley! Advance one more step, and I'll fold my anvil in two and pinch your nose with it!" John flung his own burden into the clinging mud.

The two giants stood facing off and glared into each others' wee eyes.

Matthias Crowley broke first. He sputtered. He giggled. He roared with laughter.

Laughing just as joyfully, John sloshed forward in the slippery slop to wrap around his longtime friend in a hug worthy of a bear. He stepped back two strides. You had to step back a way to see all of this hulking fellow. "Ah, Matthias, it's good to see you! It's been—how long?—seven years at least."

"Close to that. You were a lowly army centinel at Newport Pagnell, and I was an important army staff adjutant in charge of supplies and provisions."

"So that's what you called your job as the cook's helper! A turnip chopper with a title longer than his turnip tops."

Matthias shrugged cheerfully. "We are what we are." He scooped up his heavy pack. "Let's see. You live in Elstow, aye? That would be just a few miles beyond Bedford here."

"Until last year. Moved into Bedford, my wife and I. It was either move or rethatch the roof. We're less than three furlongs from my front door right now. I live in the middle of town here on St. Cuthbert's Street. You'll join my family for supper? Please!"

"Eh? You sure? I don't eat any less than I used to."

John laughed and shouldered his own pack. He led the way down the high road through Bedford town toward his little cottage on the curve. "As I recall, your appetite is what drove you to sign up as the cook's helper in the first place. Besides, my wife already knows all about your appetite. Remember we used to go along with Mad Thom to a little cottage down the road for sausages?"

Matthias nodded. "Mad Thom. What a merry bloke! And he was rather hung up on the cute little woman who made the sausages. Forget her name. Mary?" He turned wide-eyed, then crowed approvingly. "No! Splendid! How many little ones?"

"Three so far. Mary, born blind, bless her. Elizabeth. And Baby John, just born." They sloshed through the spring mud together, stride for stride, as if the space of seven years had never put a gap in their friendship.

John glanced at wee Matthias's bulk pack. "And what trade have you fallen into? I see you carrying a fair heavy bundle there."

"Y'll never guess! And it's bountifully successful, too. I'm a—hallo! What's all this?"

John stopped to watch. "So the son of consolation and thunder is back again preaching."

There in front of Bedford market, young John Burroughs yelled and waved his arms. He was preaching to a casual little knot of neighbors. John knew every one of them by name.

"Son of thunder; I can see the name." Matthias scowled. "Sounds like one of George Fox's converts. No, guess he's not. What he just said is not scriptural. Quakers claim to stick to the Bible."

"A lot of what he's saying's not scriptural." John snorted. "Remember when I was in the army, I couldn't care a penny for religion."

"Aye, I remember. John Gibbs preaching at ye time and time again, too. Wasn't he the one who broke you the news about Mad Thom? Ye know, he's the vicar of the church in Newport Pagnell now."

John grinned. "Good! Glad he put all that religion to good use!"

"So how'd you come to know the Lord, if not from the army?"

"Took years, Matthias. Long years of struggle and doubt. Am I saved or not? Did God call me out, or am I forever damned? Did I really have faith?" John jabbed Matthias's tree-trunk arm. "Let me tell you about the puddle. I was going to test my faith by telling a puddle to dry up and then couldn't get the courage. I was afraid the test answer would come out wrong!"

"What faith! I'm impressed!" The funny thing was, Matthias did not sound like he was joking. He really did sound impressed.

"I said, I didn't have the courage to try it."

"Right! You had absolute confidence that God would give you an answer one way or t'other. That's faith! Trusting God to come through."

"How I wished we had met again three years ago!" John wagged his head. "It would have saved me being tossed about. I read *Practice of Piety* cover to cover, searching. All one thousand and thirty-one pages."

"Ah, wee Johnny! Don't see how ye did it. That's the dullest, most boring book ever written in the English language."

"Know what finally set me straight? What showed me that I cannot make myself perfect, and that Jesus must do that for me? Martin Luther's commentary on Galatians. I read it, and right there I realized that God did not simply have mercy on wee Johnny Bunyan. God *wanted* to have mercy on John Bunyan. Since then I've become firm enough in the Scripture that I've even taken up preaching a little. Especially since our pastor,

John Gifford, died last year."

"Your voice tells me you were fond of this Gifford."

"Very much. He helped me overcome my doubts. He knew his Scripture. And if he were here now he wouldn't be listening to that Burroughs fellow's drivel. He'd be standing nose to nose with the lad and arguing."

"You say you've been preaching some."

"Door to door, and to small groups."

"So why aren't *you* standing nose to nose arguing with the lad?"

John stared at his burly, flamed-haired friend. Why indeed? John had never thought of himself as a speaker, really. But with Matthias Crowley at his elbow now, the one man in the army who could match him joke for joke and blow for blow, he felt bigger. More confident.

John marched forward and pushed through the little clump of listeners. He heard Matthias's huge shoes right behind him, slurping in the muddly glop.

"Say there, John Burroughs." John raised an arm. "You and your people interrupt church services regularly; now I'm interrupting you. You're not speaking the truth the way the Bible tells it there. When you talk about the divine light that is in every man you're not giving enough weight to man's sinful nature."

The stern eyes of young John Burroughs lighted up. Apparently he thrived on challenge. He restated his position. John stated his. Burroughs restated again, and they fell to arguing hotly. And all the while he argued for the Scriptures, John could feel the presence of his burly friend at his shoulder.

Matthias might grunt or mutter a cheerful, "Uh huh!" He might purr disapproval when John Burroughs misquoted Scripture. Clearly, Matthias Crowley knew the Bible inside out, and clearly he was on John's side.

Before too long, a few other people were entering the argument. It was soon very obvious that although everyone had an opinion, no one was going to change his opinion. That included John Burroughs. This argument was getting nowhere, and John was outrageously hungry. He made one last point, let others argue it, and left the group. The disagreement was still raging behind them as the two friends walked to John's cottage.

John wagged his head. "Would that the lad's knowledge matched his zeal. I wish sometimes I could simply put all these arguments on paper. Then, any man who studied the facts could see the truth right away."

"You mean quietly, apart from all this yelling."

"Exactly. The yelling and arguing sways people and keeps them from the truth."

"Then do it." Matthias chuckled. "I was going to tell you about my trade when we were distracted there. I'm a book publisher, Johnny. Not just a seller. I print them, bind them—pamphlets, tracts, broadsides, any size of books. My shop is in Newport Pagnell, but I distribute all over—including London."

"Really! And you say you're doing well."

"Aye!" Matthias stopped suddenly. "Johnny, write down the arguments you made today. They're telling arguments. Truths. You know the Scriptures as well as any man. Write it all down, and I'll have the pamphlets in your neighbors' hands by the end of the summer. I'll have them in the hands of every interested man in London, for that matter."

"Me? Write it?" John shook his head. "I'm a tinker and a preacher in equal parts, but I'm no writer. Ah, here's my cottage here, where the road curves."

Matthias shrugged, and the whole heavy pack on his back bobbed up and down. They continued on. "Write what you preach. It can't be any duller than *Practice of Piety*."

"True enough." John shifted the burden on his own back. "We could call it something simple and clear. How about *Some Gospel Truths Opened, According to the Scriptures*?"

"Splendid! Put it in my hands, and I'll do the rest. And if this John Burroughs gets a rebuttal printed, we'll print our own answer. It could keep us busy for years." Matthias clapped John on the shoulder. "And now lead me through the door to your lovely Mary and her good cooking. Aye, I remember those sausages! Feed me mortal food tonight, and tomorrow we feed the world the immortal food of God's Word!"

John paused outside his door the shortest of moments. A few minutes ago it would never have occurred to him to write anything. Now the idea seemed the most natural thing in the world. John

Bunyan the tinker was hardly a learned man, but John Bunyan the servant of God could do anything he had to in Jesus' service.

"Yes!" John pushed his cottage door open. "Mary!" he called out. "If I say 'bottomless pit,' who is the first man you think of?"

Mary had no idea who might be with John, but she didn't hesitate a second.

"Matthias Crowley."

10

The Grave in Bedford Churchyard

Spring 1659

The bells in the Bedford church steeple swung on their heavy wooden yokes, calling out the number of a woman's death. Then they began their sad and weary tolling. They counted off one by one the years of her life. Mary Bunyan, wife of John, mother of four little ones, had gone home to her father and her Father.

The world was black. All shades of black. Churning, shifting, twisting shades of black. The world swirled around him all black.

And this was no dream.

One at a time, John's friends and neighbors came to stand beside him, to lay a comforting hand on his arm, to speak a word or two. Quietly they slipped away.

The neighbor lady, a kindly widow, was keeping the children. They were so young, so tender. Blind

Mary was not quite nine, and she needed her mother more than most nine-year-olds do. The newest, baby Thomas, could not yet walk. A child that age *must* have a mother. Elizabeth was too little to manage a household, and John Junior was at the rascal age.

And John himself felt devastated. God had just snatched away the one thing John could not get through life without—his Mary.

The last of the funeral guests melted away. A heavy gray overcast made the dark day darker still. John Burton was now pastor of the Bedford congregation. He stood a few minutes beside John. A slim and sickly young man recovered from one of his frequent coughing fits, laid his hand on John's shoulder, and silently walked away. John was alone.

Mary.

John knelt beside the grave and picked up a handful of the fresh, wet dirt.

"Sir?" A voice whispered softly. "Mr. Bunyan?"

John twisted around to look.

A young girl dropped to one knee beside him. She looked perhaps seventeen or eighteen years old. Her pretty mouth turned up at the corners, as if on happy days she laughed a lot. Her face was not smiling now. She pulled her black wool cape in closer around her against the clammy cool air.

"Yes, miss?"

"I—I was all set to say something, and now I—the words all ran away. I'm sorry. But that's what I wanted to say—that I'm so sorry. Everyone says what a fine woman she was, and I heard about your children, and—" She licked her lips. "I'm so sorry. It doesn't sound very heartfelt, but it is. I mean it so very much."

John smiled in the face of his grief. "That happens to me constantly. I want to say something grand and powerful. Instead, a few weak and puny words come out—words that the wind will blow away if I don't hold onto them. I understand. Thank you." He waved a hand. "There, you see? 'Thank you' seems so flabby, and yet it means much more than it sounds like."

She studied the grass between them. "The reason I had to say something: I read your pamphlet called *A Few Sighs from Hell*. You published it last year. It helped me a great deal, because I'd been confused about certain things and—there I've lost the words again." She looked up at him, and her eyes were huge pools of blue-gray light. "I'm grateful you wrote that. It helped solve several difficult problems for me."

John stood up. "What's your name?"

"Elizabeth." She stood also.

"And where are you staying?"

"With John Grew and his wife. They's members of your congregation."

"Yes. I'll walk you back there if you wish."

"Please do." She fell in beside him as he turned his back on the newly filled grave and walked slowly off toward the high road. He opened the iron gate for her, stepping from the churchyard with all its graves into the street with all its lively people.

He looked up at the dark overcast. "When I was

growing up, everything was—well, it was quiet. Nothing changed from year to year. Solid. Stable."

"My father claimed the world resisted anything new."

"Exactly! After the civil war, when Cromwell came to power, things went all topsy-turvy. The state church and the separatists going different ways; and then the separatists splitting into so many little groups. Each group thinks he has all the truth when he holds only a tiny bit of it in his graspy little hands. It's not just religion, either. There's a whole world of new attitudes and ideas. Even new places."

"Colonies in the New World."

"New World. The Americas. New Indies. Old Indies. It's confusing, all these new things. Sometimes I wish the old solid times were back."

"Do you think everything might have become settled if Cromwell hadn't died last September?"

John studied her. Here was a girl—a very young girl—who was well informed and interesting to talk to. For some reason he could not understand, this pleased him very much. "No," he answered. "Life would have continued easier for us, no doubt, because Cromwell encouraged dissenters like ourselves. And we face bad times if those men who want to bring a king back manage to do so. But England will never go back to what she was."

"The past is gone forever?"

"Once ideas catch fire, nothing can put them out, and the country is full of new ideas. Some good, some bad, but all will change us."

"Your ideas are as new as any."

John laughed. "New? No, lass. Very old. God grants us salvation because He loves us and He wants to, and not because we can make ourselves worthy. He did it by sending His Son to the cross —something we could not do if we wanted to. He lifted the burden of sin off our backs when we could never get rid of it ourselves. That's ancient truth. Jesus and the Old Testament prophets said it centuries ago. I'm only saying it again."

She giggled. "And you say it so loudly and firmly!"

"I wasn't always so firm, you know. It took me years of arguing back and forth with myself, and of fighting with Satan."

"How do you know it was Satan?"

"Who else would beg me a hundred times to sell Jesus? 'Sell Him!' Oh, the wars in my heart that I've fought."

"And won."

"And won." He nodded. "It was a difficult time for me. For Mary, too; she had to put up with me."

They walked along in silence a few minutes. All around them busy people came and went, yet they walked together alone, just the two.

She glanced up at him bashfully. "This is all very adventuresome, you know."

"Adventuresome?"

She nodded. "I never before walked with a man who is subject to arrest. I know you were indicted last spring for preaching at Eaton, and everyone says that any time now you could be jailed again for preaching."

He chuckled. "Adventuresome. I never thought of it that way. I can't think of a better reason to go to jail than to be arrested for preaching Jesus. Of course, they have to catch me first."

"Probably what a pickpocket says every time he dips into some man's coat."

The heavy cloud of grief hung over John's head just as darkly now as it did a moment ago. And yet, here he was laughing out loud. The laughter faded. "When I knelt beside Mary's grave a few minutes ago, I was certain I could never go on. I realize now that I can, because God provides whatever I need." John raised a finger. "Not necessarily everything I *want*, understand, but all I need. You, for instance."

"Me?" Those smoky blue eyes grew wide.

"Elizabeth, young lady, you will never know what a great service you've done me today. I loved Mary so dearly. And I pray to God to help me with my grief; its burden was too heavy to carry. And He sent me you."

From the church tower the bells announced vespers to the world—as if the world did not already know it was sunset. It was the first time the bells had spoken since they tolled the number of years of Mary's short life. They spoke in sad, hushed tones. But there was hope in them, too; a gentle lilt.

The bells and John had always got on well together.

11

Dark Clouds over Bedfordshire

November 11, 1660

"Where shall I be this week, Brother Bunyan?" Elderly Mrs. Chitterling watched admiringly as John set the last of the bolts that put the handle back on her cast iron stew pot.

"Samsell. Private house."

"Near Harlington, aye. We know the place." Her gray head bobbed as enthusiastically as any teenager's. John wished all Christians were as eager for the Word as she. "Going to preach more on law and grace?"

"Aye, and I've published a pamphlet on it, if you want to send it to your cousin in Stony Stratford. *Doctrine of Law and Grace Unfolded*. The law shows us that we've sinned—"

The lady nodded even more wildly. "The law kills!"

John thought suddenly of that poor soldier so many years ago, hanged at the garrison in Newport Pagnell. "Aye, the law kills. And the opposite of law is grace, which saves us from death. And here is your good husband. G'day, Mr. Chitterling."

"G'day, Brother Bunyan!" The aged gentleman came tottering out and leaned, tilted, on both his walking stick and the gate. He looked too frail to make it across the street, and yet he and his missus walked to every meeting in the shire, no matter how far away. "Hear ye've married again."

"True! A fine young lady named Elizabeth. A beautiful gift from God to me. And you should see her eyes!"

Mrs. Chitterling absolutely glowed. "I'm so happy for you! You need a good woman—you and your little ones all."

Mr. Chitterling dug into his little purse for the tinker's payment. "William Dell up at Yelden asked you to preach his Christmas service, I hear."

"Aye. I hear it's raising quite a stink."

"A stink!" Mr. Chitterling crowed. "Some of his parishioners who don't like ye have gone so far as to petition the House of Lord to have old Dell removed from his church! Doubt they'll get very far, though. House of Lords has other things to think about these days."

John wagged his head sadly. "Wasn't long ago we could meet openly. It wasn't against the law to address God without a prayer book in your hand. Would that those who call on the name of Jesus would quit fighting among themselves and join the fight against Satan instead."

"Wouldn't it be something! Coo! Fine job ye did

on the pot there. Thank ye."

John bade them good day and started home-
ward. He'd done a long day's work. He had a long
way to travel yet, too. The days were getting short
now as winter came hurrying. November hung
heavy on the naked black trees and breathed its
cold, damp wind through their swishing
branches. John shivered despite his heavy woolen
cloak.

His oiled boots slurped in the mud as he walked
the winding road home to Bedford. Along the
roadside, the flowers of summer, once so cheery,
were dry and withered skeletons on bare stalks
now.

Half a mile short of Bedford, John met the first
person he had seen on this road for an hour.
George Mobbs was walking this way.

"Hallo, George."

"Hallo, John."

John expected George to continue on his way.
Instead, the man turned around and fell in along-
side him. They walked together in silence,
George's boots squishing in time with John's.
George's thick blond hair and droopy moustache
looked as if they were always wet, although it was
not raining just now.

"Chilly day," George began. "Looks like winter's hard on us."

"Expect so. How's the missus?"

"Fine. How's that charming bride? That Elizabeth?"

"Fine." John smiled. "A hard job for her, to
come into a household with four little children

and take over. But she's doing well, and the children like her very much."

"Good. Good. Children the age of yours can't get along without a good missus."

John nodded, and his thoughts got misty. "My own father remarried very soon after my natural mother died. I held it against him. Resented it. I can see why he did it now that I find myself doing exactly the same thing. I miss Mary so much, George. No one can ever replace her. And yet, Elizabeth is a comfort and a help to me and to the children. I love Mary, and I love Elizabeth. Strange, isn't it?"

"Nope." George had a way of clipping all the loose edges off his words. "The earthly husband and father is supposed to show us what the heavenly Father is like. And if our heavenly Father could only love one of us at a time, a whole lot of us would be out of luck."

John laughed. "How true."

"Speaking of luck," George continued. "I hear you're preaching at Harlington on Christmas and at Samsell tomorrow night."

"That's right."

"Ye might think twice about it. I hear a rumor from a good source that there's a warrant out for your arrest the next time you open your mouth."

"I've been threatened before and brought before the magistrates a time or two. I wouldn't worry."

"I would." George's voice took on a sharp edge. "I asked a friend of mine about the business. His name's Paul Cobb, and he fancies himself an expert on the law. I suspect he is, too, because he's the clerk to the justices. He claims a law on the books from back in Queen Elizabeth's day is being used now against dissenters. If you don't go to the state's church in the space of a month, or if you attend an unlawful assembly—"

"Which is what we're doing."

"Right. You're imprisoned without bail until you show up in church and confess to the error of your ways. The third offense and you're sent to prison until assizes. If they find you guilty they ship you clear out of England for seven years, and if you show up in the country before those seven years are up, they hang you."

"Costly way for the state to get rid of dissenters."

"Not really. They sell your house and land for the money to buy your boat trip to the ends of the earth, and then they keep the change."

"Not every dissenter owns a house and land they could sell."

"Then they indenture you to the ship's captain as a slave for five years or else sell your wife and children into service. Cobb spelled it out for me."

"Oh, come!" John fumed. "All that trouble for an insignificant little country preacher like me?"

"Ye don't realize what a danger ye are. Hundreds of people flock to hear you preach. And those pamphlets you write are powerful."

John sniffed. "Who signed the warrant for my arrest, do you know?"

"Justice Wingate, I hear. Lawyer Foster here in Bedford is in on it; so's Vicar Lindale. You have lots of enemies."

"Only one that I fear—Satan. Thank you for the warning, but I promised to preach tomorrow at Samsell, and I shall."

"Wish ye wouldn't."

They were coming into Bedford town now. The houses, which usually looked so open and friendly, frowned this evening. John and George walked in silence, passing door after closed door.

Here was George's little house. He stopped at his gate, so John stopped. He shook John's hand. "I realize ye must do the Lord's will, but if it were my will I'd say stay home with your pretty bride and let someone else rot in jail."

"Appreciate it, brother. Thank you. God bless you."

"And ye, too, Brother Bunyan." That rough, hard hand gave John's an extra squeeze. Then George pushed through his narrow little front gate and walked up the path to his own dark door.

John walked on. Somehow his load of tools and anvil seemed much heavier. Here was his own door. It looked just as dark as any other. He pushed it open.

Blind Mary, almost eleven, sat by the warmth of the hearth working on a basket. Her natural mother had taught her to weave rushes, and now Elizabeth was teaching her to knit lace. The blind knitting lace? Marvelous! Elizabeth was also teaching Mary how to get out and around almost as well as any sighted person.

Little Liz was clearing the table. She scurried about very importantly. Until John remarried, she had been the mama of the house. The burden of three small children is much too heavy for a nine-year-old, but she had done well. Very well.

And there was three-year-old John in the middle of the floor. He always filled up the middle of the floor. He was talking a blue streak to no one in particular as he built a castle out of bits and ends of boards. When he grew up, would he face the same persecutions and dangers his father was facing now? John must work to give his sons an easier time.

Elizabeth sat by the hearth breaking potatoes up into little pieces for two-year-old Thomas. She looked up at John and smiled. It was a sad smile, and wary. "Did George Mobbs find you?"

"Aye. We talked." He glanced at the children.

She nodded. One does not discuss arrest out loud in front of the children. "Your supper will be ready. I thought I'd feed the children first and put them to bed."

"Fine." John shed his burden with a sigh and left anvil, tools, and all in a heap by the door. The teapot was still hot. He poured himself a cup and sprawled in the wooden settle beside the fire, utterly spent.

Elizabeth wiped off Thomas's goopy face. "Still preaching tomorrow?"

"Aye."

She said nothing more. She helped John Junior clean up his blocks. She brushed out Mary's long dark hair. She ushered each child to bed and listened to prayers. Her duties as a mother done, she returned to the hearth and stirred whatever it was (and it smelled delicious!) that bubbled in the iron pot.

John watched her face a few moments and reached out to lay a hand on her arm. She sat down at his feet, her legs curled up beneath her, and laid her head on his knee. Red flecks of firelight glittered in her eyes. She was near to crying. "I'm afraid, John."

"So am I."

"Must you preach?"

"I said I would. Therefore I must."

"If you stopped preaching just a couple months, this nasty business might blow over. Maybe the magistrates will get involved in other problems and forget about you."

"Our public servants the magistrates are not so easily distracted. Just last month they passed the law requiring a certain way of worship, and they're anxious to use it. No Elizabeth, it's not going to get any better. Especially not with Charles Second coming to the throne. The royalists are against us, and they're in power now."

She shivered, although the room was not cold.

He rubbed her shoulder. "We've always had that threat—that little cloud—over our heads. It's simply that the cloud's a bit darker now."

"Remember when I said I thought it was adventuresome to be with a man who might get arrested?"

"I remember."

"Sure didn't know much then, did I?"

12

An Arrest in Samsell

November 12, 1660

Fox and hounds. The hounds pursue the fox, as the fox tries to prove he is smarter than the dogs. The sleek foxhounds, all groomed and elegant, run in packs yipping and calling. They follow their quarry not with their eyes but with their keen noses. The fox, all tawny red, tries a hundred tricks to fool the hounds into thinking he is someplace he is not. To the hounds it is a lively game. To the fox, it is a deadly game.

John Bunyan, burly and tawny-haired, considered himself the fox. The royalists were those hounds yipping at his heels just one step behind him. To elude the hounds, John preached in strange places at strange times. It might be on Coleman Green up in Sandridge one week, or Wainwood Dell near Hitchin the next. He liked preaching in the shed at Bendish; it had a handy escape door out the back. And there was this huge and lovely old tree in a meadow under which John would preach now and then; already people were startling to call it Tinker's Hill.

Tonight the place would be a private house in Samsell. All the dissenters knew where the meeting would be. But did the hounds know? There were spies among the foxes; everyone knew that.

Ah, well. God saw what he was doing. If God did not approve, God would remove John Bunyan. And if God did approve, all the magistrates in England could not stop the preaching of the Word. John must depend upon God.

He walked the last quarter mile, down through the quiet little village, and knocked at the door.

Sister Ruth opened it. She was a frail little lady, no doubt twenty years older than the age of forty that she admitted to. "Here you are." Her voice dropped a notch. "We wouldn't blame you if you stayed away. You heard?"

"I heard. May I come in?"

"Oh, of course! Of course!" Flustered and embarrassed, she stepped aside for him.

Tables and chairs had been pushed back against the walls, and people sat on both. More people sat on the floor. The room was filled. Every face here was familiar to John. Most of them had been his customers at one time or another. All of them trusted Jesus for their salvation.

A few more believers came trickling in, making the crowded room more crowded still. The worshipers giggled together and traded news, for most had not seen each other since the last meeting. But the small talk tonight was not as merry as usual. A dark cloud hung over this meeting—a dread.

In the far distance, the bells of the church in Harlington called vespers. "The day is ended," said the bells.

"Brothers and sisters, let us begin." John raised his hands. The chatter stilled.

Heavy fists pounded on the door. The roomful gasped as one. Every head swung to stare at the door, wide-eyed.

John kept his voice low and even; it was a chore, too. "God calls us in Hebrews to not neglect gathering together. Therefore we are in His will, and Jesus says where two or three are gathered, there He is among them. We are in divine company. Let us speak to our Lord first in silent prayer.';

More pounding.

Her hands shaking like aspen leaves in a high wind, Sister Ruth started for the door, but it flew open before she could get there. The Harlington constable came striding in all awash with authority.

"You are interrupting communion with God, sir," John snapped sternly.

"And not a *Book of Common Prayer* in sight, either. All the worse for you. I have here the warrant signed by Justice Wingate. I arrest you in the name of the crown, John Bunyan of Bedford."

So. The worst had come. All Elizabeth's wishes that the problems would disappear, all John's hopes that this might not happen—all that was gone, dissolved in the gush of rain from that breaking cloud. John could only pray now that he would provide a strong and dignified example for these other believers.

"Come along!" the constable barked.

John knew the passage of Scripture that applied here. Even as the constable laid his hand on John's arm, John was thumbing through his Bible to Romans 13.

" 'Let every soul be subject to the higher powers,' " John read, " 'for there is no power but of God; the powers that be are ordained of God.' "

The constable was pulling on his arm now, dragging him toward the door. He read on. " 'Whosoever therefore that resists the power resists the ordinance of God. And they that resist shall receive to themselves damnation.' "

The door slammed shut behind him, and they were walking in frigid blackness. He closed his Bible and tucked it under his arm. They cut across Sulross's Lane to the main road.

John frowned. "This isn't the way to the jail."

"I'm to take you to Justice Wingate's house. His orders."

Frozen on the surface and soft underneath, the road gave a little beneath each step. How long yet would he walk in free air? Was this another of those arrests where they trotted him before a magistrate, lectured him, and sent him on? Apparently not this time. This time they were out to silence him for good.

Justice Wingate's house appeared dark as they approached. No light slipped between the shutters. No smoke floated up from the chimney. The constable rapped loudly at the door. If the man had a gift from God it was his ability to pound on doors.

No one came. Minutes passed. John was starting to get cold, standing here like this. The constable scowled at him in the darkness, as if John were somehow responsible.

The constable thumped on the door again and waited. He snorted. "The old coot knew I'd be by with you. Told me to come. Now he's not home." He wheeled and waggled a finger in John's face. "With a warrant on you there's nowhere to run. You know that. So get on home, and I'll come fetch you in the morning to appear before the justice. Go now."

John felt like a lamb led to slaughter only to watch the ax pause. The ax would fall, no doubt, but not tonight. "I shall do as the Lord commands. Good night, constable." John hurried off into the darkness, lest the man change his mind. Even more than the constable, John was accustomed to traveling at night, for his tinkering trade often left him far from home at nightfall.

He walked rapidly along the narrow winding roads he had known since childhood. His own hands now were trembling almost as wildly as Sister Ruth's. He entered Bedford by the back lane. The Simmons dog barked from across the alley. Jane's dog took up the call from the other street. Those two great mastiffs of Sister Harmon's woofed; they sounded as if they were right at his heels, and he knew they were two streets away.

He popped out onto St. Cuthbert's Street, turned thirty paces to the right, and entered the door of his own cottage.

He expected Elizabeth to be asleep. Instead she sat by the hearth watching the tired red embers of the dying fire. She jumped when he came through the door.

She stood up to greet him. "You're back early."

He shrugged out of his heavy woolen cloak. "Come put your arms around an arrested man, Mrs. Bunyan, and join him in a prayer for tomorrow."

Her pretty head pressed against his chest. "What now?" She whispered. "Do you know?"

He hugged her tightly. "No. Perhaps another scolding, perhaps a fine, perhaps a few days in jail. We have enough money aside to keep you and the children going for a couple weeks. And God will come up with what we need from then on."

John hoped his voice sounded casual and confident. He himself certainly did not. Yes, he trusted his Lord. Yes, he knew God's will would be done.

But in spite of all these things he knew with his head, fear still tied his heart into twisted knots.

What lay ahead?

13

The County Jail in Bedford Town

November 13, 1660

He looked like a man who had been born weary. His eyelids drooped at half mast. His cheeks sagged, dragging the corners of his mouth into a constant downward grump. The outside corners of his eyes sagged, too, putting his whole pudgy face on a subtle downhill slide. Justice Francis Wingate peered at John Bunyan through gray and watery eyes and droned, "Who declares against this man?"

Dr. Lindale, the aging vicar from Harlington, read the charges. He used just about the same words George Mobbs had quoted two days ago. That Paul Cobb fellow must know what he was talking about.

John glanced toward the back of the room. Elizabeth and all four children sat tensely, quietly. Not even little Tom was fidgeting.

"And who examines this man?" Justice Wingate sounded bored, but John knew better. The justice hated dissenters and loved causing them problems.

"I shall examine." Lawyer Foster stood up. "John Bunyan, numerous witnesses testify that you have been heard preaching at gatherings and on the road from house to house. Have you training in theology?"

"My learning comes from the study of the divine Word, the Bible."

"Answer the question asked," Justice Wingate drawled.

"I did so, your honor," John replied. "I have no degree from a theology school, but I have trained myself." John had been through all these questions and answers more than once. So had the justice and lawyer Foster—the vicar also, no doubt. John was not the first dissenter hauled before a court like this, nor was it his first time. Usually, though, it was village magistrates who snapped and snarled and chewed on him.

He glanced back again at Elizabeth. Poor Elizabeth. John might be used to these goings-on, but she was not. She looked pale and worried.

"You have a calling," Justice Wingate, was saying. "Tinkering. Follow it."

"I have two callings and follow both—tinkering and preaching."

"You're ignorant and not a fit preacher!"

"God chose the foolish to confound the wise."

"No one listens to you but ignorant, foolish people!"

"Then, ignorant and fool, the greater they need to be taught. God has called me to spread the good news to His people—"

"But not by a man called to be a tinker."

"—and I will not leave off preaching."

"Enough!" Justice Wingate lurched forward and his droopy face sagged even further. "Your guilt is clear, tinker Bunyan. I remand you to the county jail until seven weeks from now. You will be tried then at the sessions to be held in the Chapel of Herne, near the grammar school, commonly called Schoolhouse Chapel. Away with him, constable."

The constable turned John around and gave him a shove toward the doors. It was over that quickly—just a few questions, a few arguments, and now John would spend seven weeks in jail! How could Satan win so easily when God's people seemed to have such trouble winning anything at all? Ah, well, Jesus called His believers to persecution, didn't He?

Elizabeth, pale and shaking, watched him pass. Her cheeks were wet, her lips a thin, white little line.

The walk from Justice Wingate's house to the jail took a bit less than an hour and a half. John listened to every leaf rustle. He heard a crow in the cow pasture beside the road and envied its freedom. Seven weeks! The punishment was more than John would have expected. He surely must seem dangerous to his enemies.

John had not had much to do with jails in his life, other than to walk past them frequently.

There was the county jail built of stone, here in Bedford. And there was the village jail, a little stone box built right on the Swan Bridge over the river. In the little jail were kept people convicted of minor offenses—drunkenness and such.

John was ushered into the big jail, the county jail. The heavy armored door thudded shut behind him. This might be the larger of the two jails, but there were still more prisoners than prison. Every little cell was crowded, for the justices had made quite free about jailing dissenters lately. But then, the beds were nothing more than a pile of straw on the dirt floor, so there was always room for one more. The cell door clanged behind him, and John was in what would be his home for the next seven weeks.

Six other men lived in this small cell. Only one tiny window set high in the wall let in air and light. It was barred for no good purpose; not even a cat could squeeze through it comfortably. There was a tax on windows, and the jail paid its taxes just like everyone else.

John's cellmates huddled in one great ill-clad heap, trying to keep each other warm. In summer, one might resent the appearance of still another prisoner in this tiny room. Now, in November, another warm body was welcome. John saw no fire anywhere in this building, and he could not remember whether the jail even had a chimney.

The jailer called in through the barred door: "Water's in the courtyard. Your food will be a quarter loaf of bread daily plus whatever your family happens to bring you. Your wife said some-

thing about sending over a pot of soup each day."
And the fellow left.

Here were six other men, and still John felt utterly alone. He had no wife, no children, no
friends and—it seemed so, almost—not even a
God to comfort him. He was feeling just a little bit
the way Jesus must have felt as He was being
nailed to the cross. Abandoned.

Nonsense! John's situation was nothing like
that at all. He had his Bible under his arm. He
would keep himself busy. The time would pass.
He sat down among the huddled cellmates.

He found himself listening. For what? Bells.
That was it. Perhaps there was a wedding, or even
a funeral. Something. But the bells were silent.

They had abandoned him, too.

14

The Sentence at
Schoolhouse Chapel

January 1661

The Chapel at Herne near the grammar school
didn't look much like a chapel at all, either inside
or outside. The inside was bland and faceless with
no carvings, no statues, no pictures, no colored
windows. It was designed to be all things to all
men.

Do you need a court for the justices to meet?
Here it is. Do the magistrates need a place to sit
on an afternoon? Here it is. Does the vicar down
the road want to hold a quiet little funeral for a
known sinner? Let him hold it here. Benches, tables, chairs, and even the altar were loose; they
could be moved around freely to suit whatever
purpose the latest user might have.

Today it was the justices. They sat at the front
of the hollow room at great benches, from there to
scowl down at the world. There would be no jury

for cases against dissenters. The jury box, such as it was, had been rearranged into benches for the accused persons and for those who cared to watch the court in action.

John sat on a bench against the wall and looked over the row of justices who would hear his case.

He saw trouble immediately. If Justice Wingate hated dissenters, Justice Kelynge loathed them utterly. And Justice Kelynge presided. There were Sir William Beecher and Sir Henry Chester, all wrapped up in their own importance. John remembered someone's saying that those two gentlemen considered it their duty to squash dissenters. Sir George Blundell of Cardington John had met before; the man was bitterly against any religious nonconformity. Thomas Snagg from over at Millbrook was no friend of dissenters, either. John could not see a friendly face in the whole room, save Elizabeth's.

She sat near the back as before, with the children huddled close against her. John smiled at her across the room. He tried to say with his smile, *Be brave. This will all be over soon.*

One by one the prisoners, most of them dissenters, were hauled before Justice Kelynge. Some of them were Quakers. John was strongly against some of the views of Quakers, but he hated seeing them arrested. He should be free to worship and preach as he wished, and so should they. And so, then must the Episcopalians and the Presbyterians and the Anabaptists and all the others who called upon Jesus be free.

He heard his name and already the bailiff was

reading off the charges against him: "—devilishly and perniciously abstained from coming to church to hear divine service and is a common upholder of several unlawful meetings and conventicles—"

Devilish in a pig's eyes! John was the enemy of Satan!

"—contrary to the laws of our sovereign lord the King."

If the king was so sovereign a lord, John mused, why did heaven not collapse when Charles the First, as sovereign as any, was beheaded eleven years ago?

Justice Kelynge peered out from under his judicial wig. "Do you come to parish church to hear divine service?"

"No, I do not."

"Why?"

"I did not find it commanded in the Word of God. The Word tells us not to neglect meeting together. It says nothing about a steeplehouse. Jesus said, 'Where two or three are—' "

"Your meetings do not follow the *Book of Common Prayer*. We are commanded to pray."

"But not by the common prayer book."

"How then?"

"With the Spirit."

For some reason John's lively defense did not impress Justice Kelynge. In fact it seemed to make the bewigged justice quite angry. The other men behind the bench were none too pleased, either. They fell to shouting and arguing amongst themselves. Their knowledge of basic Bible truths seemed sadly lacking, and John corrected some points. That didn't sit too well either.

"Silence!" Justice Wingate shrieked, and the world fell silent. "Your words convict you even if the testimony and your reputation did not. I remand you to prison for three months. If at three months' end you do not submit to go to church to hear divine service, and leave off your preaching, you must be banished from the realm. And if, after such a day as shall be appointed you to be gone, you shall be found in this realm, or be found to come over again without special license from the king, you must stretch by the neck for it. I tell you plainly. Away with him, jailer."

John stood speechless. He could not believe a judge would render so severe a sentence, not even a judge who hated dissenters.

Clear and loud, blind Mary's voice piped up from the back of the room. "What does it mean, Mama? Banished from the realm?"

"It means he must leave England forever. If he comes back, they will hang him." Elizabeth's voice broke.

Already the chief justice was hearing the charges against the next prisoner. The constable was leading John away, back to prison.

Three months! And then? John could not stop his preaching. He knew that much. He certainly didn't have the money to buy passage out of England, and he absolutely would not let them sell the roof from over Elizabeth's head. He would not let them steal his children's birthright and land; the Bunyans had been here more than four hundred years! Rather his children should be orphaned than that.

Orphaned! For their father would surely hang. John was bringing so much suffering upon Elizabeth and the children! And yet, God permitted all this, and God's will must be done. He said that over and over to himself as he was thrust back into that familiar little cell.

The only piece of furniture in the cell was a rickety ladder-back chair. John pulled it over to the outside wall. By standing on it he could just see out the window. He steadied himself by gripping the iron bars. The iron, chilled to January's temperature, sapped the warmth from his hand and left it painfully cold.

A dark, bare grove of ash trees rose above the roof beyond the jail. How many times had he walked past that grove as he plied his trade? He was not a tinker because his father was. He was a tinker because he loved being a tinker. He made a good living, and he was strong enough that he did not mind carrying those heavy tools about. Most of all he loved walking up and down the countryside, talking to all those people, talking about his Lord.

How could he sit in this cell for three months? He was used to walking miles. Here he could go only four paces before he had to turn around. The air was clammy and thick, for only this one small window provided ventilation.

He missed Elizabeth and the children already.

In the mists beyond, he could barely see the hills between Bedford and Elstow. He remembered climbing the highest of them with Margaret those many years ago when he was fifteen. Margaret. He missed them all—his beloved Mary, his mother, Margaret. So many.

Someone was getting married up in the church, for St. Cuthbert's bells began to ring. There was joy somewhere. Not here.

John climbed down from the chair and sat in the gloom. He listened with tears to his friends the bells—pealing, leaping, singing so wild and free.

15

Determination by Firelight

February 1661

Elizabeth sighed a long shuddering sigh. She nestled her head tighter against him. John pulled her close, even though she was already pressed as close as she could be. They had pulled the settle, that high-backed wooden chair John's father had made for them, around to face the fireplace. John watched the red coals around the edge flicker and flare. He watched the burning log send up its licking little flames of yellow and orange. It was so fine to be able to sit close enough to a fire to feel its warmth and to be hypnotized by its fluid dance.

Someone knocked at the door. Elizabeth sat bolt upright and stared at John. Her eyes were wide pools of fear.

"Mrs. Bunyan? It's Paul Cobb, the justice clerk." The voice outside spoke hesitantly.

John squeezed her hand. Slowly she stood. Cautiously she crossed to the door. She opened it the barest bit. "Yes, Mr. Cobb?"

"I understand you traveled to London to appeal your husband's sentence. I apologize for the late hour, but I'm anxious to hear how your trip went. May I come in?"

Elizabeth looked at John across the room. He nodded. She opened the door and stepped back.

Mr. Cobb walked two steps inside and stopped. His mouth dropped open. "John Bunyan! You're supposed to be in prison! How did you escape?"

John smiled and waved an arm. "Come in, Mr. Cobb. Please sit. Elizabeth, a pot of hot tea would go down nicely."

Paul Cobb was a small man, slight and scrawny, but he would have looked a little larger if he didn't hunch over so. Perhaps he had been working on ledgers and books a bit too long. He took a careful seat on the edge of the chair Elizabeth provided him.

"The jailer and I have become good friends," John explained. "I help him in the day-to-day running of the place, and for a small consideration he occasionally leaves the door ajar, so to speak. He's a good person; he could get into a lot of trouble for letting me go now and then."

"So you can come see your wife."

"And so I can preach."

Paul Cobb's eyes bulged wide enough to reflect the orange fireglow. "Surely you don't preach in public!"

"At meetings of believers. Yes. It's my calling."

"But—but—" Mr. Cobb sank back into the chair and wagged his head. The firelight made his skin look warmer than it appeared in daylight. "You do something so insane, even as your wife is suffering on your behalf! And, Mr. Bunyan, as I am working on your behalf. Mrs. Bunyan, did you get to see the Earl of Bedford at all?"

"Yes," she said quietly.

"Well? Did he seem at all sympathetic?"

She stood beside the hearth and never had she seemed so tall and proud. "I left the children in the care of a neighbor and traveled for three days to London to find the earl's offices. I explained to him—to them; there were others with him—about our state and about how John had never done a dishonest thing. I described John's character. They laughed at him. They ridiculed him—and me. John can argue with important men, but I'm afraid I'm just a country girl. I couldn't argue, but I did plead. They wouldn't listen. They chased me away."

"They drove her away in tears," John corrected.

"No, Mr. Cobb. No sympathy there."

"I'm sorry, Mrs. Bunyan. And more than a little ashamed of the earl." Mr. Cobb studied the fire awhile, captured by its magic just as John had been. "Oh. Thank you." He accepted a cup of tea. Elizabeth brought John one and curled up beside him on the settle with her own.

"I won't see my family made poor and homeless," said John. "I'll be freed, or I'll be hanged, but not deported."

"You don't have to sound so—so doomed."

"I *am* doomed, Mr. Cobb. So I will preach as long as I can and then—" John spread his hands helplessly. "The earl was about our last hope."

"This is ridiculous," Mr. Cobb exploded. "All you have to do is show up at St. Cuthbert's now and then and stop preaching awhile. Instead of preaching, write anonymously. You already publish pamphlets, George tells me."

"Writing and preaching aren't the same at all. I'm called to preach. Either God will deliver me so I can continue preaching, or I will die in His will and service."

Mr. Cobb grimaced. "You seem delighted to make enemies of people in high places."

"Enemies! My enemies call me ignorant, yet I know the Scriptures well, and they do not. They call me a fool, yet they blindly oppose God as He is revealed through His Word; that's the ultimate foolishness. They say I am dangerous, yet it is they who persecute honest men."

Mr. Cobb's eye met John's. "They're afraid; that's all. Afraid of change."

"Can you remember when there was no tea?" John lifted his cup.

"When I was a child." Mr. Cobb smiled. "Tea became the rage when I was very small."

"And I. When I entered the army no one had ever heard of it, and when I came out everyone was drinking it. My father sips his tea now and mutters, 'I can't imagine how we got along without it.' The justices drink just as much tea as we do, and their fathers were just as ignorant of it as ours were. It's not change they're afraid of. They're afraid if fewer people go to the state church, the church will have less power and will give them less support. Royalists and separatists, just like always."

"I suspect you're right. But that doesn't help you."

"No, nor does it serve our Lord." John sighed patiently. "Mr. Cobb, three months ago I would have been tempted to do as you suggest, just to save my family any more grief. But I've grown in jail. Lots of time to study Scripture. Peter was delivered from prison. Paul in Rome was not. God picks and chooses what He wants, and He's handling everything. I'm going to keep doing what He wants and let Him do with me whatever He wants."

"And there's no way I can talk sense into you?"

John smiled. "I must do what I must do."

"Then so must I. I'll work toward your release, but I have very little hope anything will come of my efforts." Paul Cobb stood up. "Thank you for tea, Mrs. Bunyan. Again I apologize about the earl. Good night, John Bunyan."

John stood up. "Good night. And thank you for your help. And your sympathy towards Elizabeth."

Elizabeth closed the door after Mr. Cobb left. She dropped the bar and leaned against the door a few moments. She crossed back to John and wrapped her frail arms around his waist. She sighed from a depth that jarred John's soul. His head had known all along how much she put up with. But now for the first time his heart found out.

And the sudden wrenching ache was almost more than he could stand.

16

A Coffin at St. Cuthbert's

Spring 1666

It came suddenly, without warning. You felt hot, then cold, then hot, then cold. You ached all over. Hard knots bulged under your armpits and where your legs meet your body. Sometimes those painful lumps, called buboes, broke into open sores. Often you died before they had time to. If the plague stayed in those lumps, and if you were very, very lucky, you might be the one in five who got the disease and lived. The other four would be dead in a day. If the plague entered your lungs you were certain to die.

The bubonic plague, called simply the plague, had always been a threat. A few centuries ago it had wiped out a fourth of the people in Europe. Many people died from it every year. But 1665 and into 1666 was the year when the plague ran wild. In that year's time, 75,000 people died just in London town.

You feared the army that invaded, but at least

you knew where it was and could count its strength. Ah, but fear of the plague—that was a far more savage fear. The plague was invisible and much stronger than any army. It invaded silently; it struck where and when it wanted. It feasted on grief and turned to strike again.

Terrified people hid in their homes; the plague slipped through locked doors. Each night the dead were carried away by the cartload. Often, though, those who were not too sick to bury the dead were afraid to touch the bodies. Many doctors fled the cities where they were needed most.

The people who normally loved blood sports stayed away from the Bear Garden, where men teased bears into fighting and pitted dogs against raging bulls. The Globe and Blackfriars Theatres stood empty; no one came anymore to watch the plays of Shakespeare and Marlowe. For month upon month the smell of death hung as heavy as the fear in the streets of London. The bells tolled constantly.

John Bunyan sat in his dank cell in Bedford jail, as helpless as everyone else. He could read his Bible and pray for his family. That was all. Was it enough? Though the plague hit London hardest, it was striking here in the small towns, too. No one was safe.

The jailer stuck his head in the cell door. "Johnny? Man to see you."

John grunted. As he stood, the jailer added, "Bring your cloak" and walked off, leaving the door open. John remembered to close it behind him.

He stepped toward the front door and stopped, scowling.

Paul Cobb, the justice clerk, wasn't smiling either. He stood in the outside doorway. "John."

"Paul."

Paul Cobb shuffled from foot to foot. "Guess you heard how bad things are getting. The vicar at Stony Stratford is gone. Elstow Church opens once a month because the pastor there has to divide his time between that and three other villages. The high roads haven't been attended to since last spring. The Swan Bridge is ready to fall down it needs repair so badly. There's no one left to handle burials at St. John's. We need a couple bell ringers, too."

"Little Mary brings me the news along with my soup each day. I hear."

"Your religion doesn't at all suit the magistrates, but they need your strong back. They told me to release you so you can help out around town."

"Not released honorably, with a pardon. Just turned loose to work for them like a horse or ox."

"They're desperate, John," Paul said softly. "They haven't softened toward dissenters. Soon as the emergency's past and the plague quiets down, you can be sure they'll slap you back in jail. But we need you now."

"I almost rather sit here and let you sweat, but my Lord Jesus called me to serve all men as if I were serving Him personally. Therefore I must." John turned to the jailer. "Am I free?"

"You're free." The jailer waved a paper. "Go

home to your good wife."

Paul did not move out of the doorway.

John threw his heavy cloak over his shoulders. "Make up a list of things that must be done, most urgent ones first. I'll see what I can do."

Still Paul did not move. "I hear you published another pamphlet with Charles Doe."

"A book this time. *Grace Abounding to the Chief of Sinners*."

The jailer waved a copy. "It's the story of his conversion. How he grew in the faith. And he wrote it right here in my jail!"

Paul smiled grimly. "Say anything in there about praying for your enemies?"

"Of course we must pray for our enemies. But that makes them no less our enemies."

"And you think I'm your enemy. Elizabeth said so."

"Five years ago when King Charles was crowned, they set thousands of prisoners free. Coronation amnesty. I was not among them."

"Nearly everyone who was free had not been tried yet. You had been tried and found guilty."

"But then I tried to get my name on the calendar of felons to be tried. I asked the judge and the sheriff. I wrote letters. But you scratched my name off the jailer's list and insisted I not be tried as a felon. Yes, I found out about it. Is that what a friend would do?"

"Yes, it is!" Paul snapped. "The coronation amnesty put a freeze on hangings and deportations. It gave you a year's grace period because convicts must have time to file appeals. If you had drawn attention to yourself by showing up in court you would have certainly been deported or hanged. You might not like their charges, but you're guilty of them, all of same. Elizabeth understands that. Why can't you?"

"Five years away from my family while other men walk free!"

"You aren't alone. John Donne's still in here. He was supposed to be shipped off to Barbados years ago. It's your stubbornness that kept you in here those five years. If you'd just bend a little—"

"The truth must never be bent. Excuse me." John was burly enough that he could have simply walked out the door, for Paul Cobb was a slight man. He waited, though, until Paul had stepped aside.

The sun slapped John's face. Free! He hurried up the street toward home. Did Elizabeth know he was coming? Probably. Paul Cobb seemed to be keeping her informed.

Just as he approached the church the bells began to ring. He stopped. They rang the number of a man. And now the deep bell started its tolling. Here came the funeral procession out the huge church doors and down the steps. The bell tolled on. John counted the strokes with part of his mind while the other part watched the widow with her veiled face.

The great bell stopped and by stopping made the silence ring. Thirty-eight slow bongs. Why, John Bunyan was exactly thirty-eight! And here he stood, healthy and well, watching the coffin of a man less fortunate than himself.

So John Bunyan pitied himself for spending five weary years in prison, did he? He had put the time to good use. He had been making tagged shoelaces for Elizabeth to sell; it wasn't tinkering, but it was certainly income. He had written a book and a series of pamphlets, all to help people know God better.

He was almost comfortable in jail, he had been there so long. He had a stool to sit on and a flute to play at odd moments, whittled from a chair leg. He had his little writing table given to him by John Donne, who suffered just as much as he. He could study; he could write; he could preach to his fellow prisoners. He had it better than many men and infinitely better than the fellow passing by him in a box just now. It was only by God's good grace that John was watching this coffin and not riding in it.

He continued up the street to his cottage. Little Mary was not so little now. At sixteen she was as lithe and pretty as her mother had been. She sat on the cottage doorstep now with her legs tucked up tight, grasshopperlike. John stopped a moment to watch her before she heard him. Like many blind people she rocked back and forth without realizing it. Her hand waved back and forth in front of her face, as if she were keeping a pesky fly at bay. She was strong and weather-tanned, and she could get around town like any sighted person, for it was she who brought John his soup each day.

Sixteen years old. So many things had happened in those sixteen years! John ordered his legs into action again.

Mary sat up straight, her head tilted. She jumped to her feet. "Mama! He's back! Papa?" She stood up and came walking rapidly toward him without hesitating, without groping. He spoke her name so she would know for certain it was he, and when she reached him they hugged tightly.

The other children came tumbling out the front door to greet him.

A short time ago John had been angry all over again with Paul Cobb. A shorter time ago the sight of that funeral had opened his eyes to his own faults. Now he knew he must go apologize to Paul for not forgiving him years ago. He must apologize to God for being such a crab when he was actually being treated quite well. But all that was for later.

Right now, his heart was singing.

The sun and the breeze and his children surrounded him and escorted him home.

17

The Barn in Ruffhead's Orchard

September 1671

"Soup's here, Johnny!" The jailer opened the cell door.

John laid his pen aside and stood up from his table. Elizabeth stood in the doorway with his soup jug. As he left his cell the jailer closed the door behind him. John wrapped his burly arm around Elizabeth's shoulders and escorted her out into the jail courtyard. They sat down together under a crippled old oak tree.

John popped the lid on his soup jug and slurped a spoonful of perfectly marvelous lamb stew. "Mary isn't ill, I hope."

Elizabeth beamed. "She's found work! They say her sense of touch is so keen she'll be a splendid wool carder and spinner. She's very happy for the chance. And your father's been taking Thomas around with him as an apprentice, more or less, since he can't go out and about with you. He's using your anvil."

"Good. Good. How's baby Sarah?"

"Over the croup and doing fine." Elizabeth usually sat watching John while he ate. Today she stared at his boots, all wrapped up in the world within herself.

John paused to chew a bit on a chunk of turnip. "You're quiet. What's wrong?"

"Nothing. Children are fine. I'm fine."

"You're quiet. What's wrong?" Hungry as he was, he abandoned his stew to watch her face. It told him plainly that she was fretting.

She looked at him a moment and let her eyes slide away. "The people in the Bedford meeting elected themselves a pastor yesterday."

"Really! Who?"

"You."

John laughed out loud. "They elected a jailbird for a pastor! They must think I'm getting out soon."

"You've been coming and going rather freely for the last year." She faced him squarely. "John, I don't like it. I'm frightened."

"I've been in jail here—off and on—for over eleven years now. What more can they do to me?"

"I'll tell you what they can do! You remember what happened a year ago in May. John Fenne! And Nehemiah Cox. Arrested and fined over sixty pounds, and when we couldn't scrape the money together they sold everything John owned. Everything! He and his family are destitute. They have to depend on whatever the congregation can spare for them."

"I know that."

"And Brother Prynne, and Burton, and Bost-wick—got holes bored in their ears for attending meetings. Not preaching, mind you; just attending. And do you know that three believers were hanged over in—"

"Yes, I know!"

"But you don't understand how I worry—" she wailed.

"Elizabeth. They aren't going to hang me, or they would've done it by now. I don't even think they'll deport me, or they'd have done that. They sentenced John Donne to deportation to Barbados years ago, and he's still in jail here with me. It's easing up, Elizabeth. The jailer's been letting me go out for a day or two at a time during this last year because he knows it's easing. Those horrible things you were just talking about—that was one last fling, you might say. The magistrates' last try to stomp us out. It didn't work. There are more dissenters than ever. And they're realizing that. It's getting better."

"You've been saying it's getting better for twelve years."

"No, you've been hoping it's getting better. Now it really is."

"I'm sorry. For five years we haven't been able to write anything into the church record for fear the wrong people will find it. We hide like mice from a cat."

"Like a fox from the hounds. I know. Be patient. Be brave."

She sighed and pulled her knees up. She rested her chin on her knees and stared at something a million miles away. "I suppose this all means that you'll accept the position as pastor when they offer it."

"Yes, I will." John abandoned his soup for the moment to reach out and rub her shoulder. "We tell the children to depend on God and follow Jesus. Doesn't do much good to preach that to them if we don't follow it ourselves."

She sighed heavily. "I know. But I still don't like it."

He chuckled. "We don't have to like the orders; we only have to follow them."

Easy to say. So hard to do.

John's prediction turned out to be right. Early in 1672, a proclamation called the Act of Indulgence made church meetings outside the state church not exactly legal but more respectable. In May of 1672 John and twenty-five other dissenters were granted licenses to preach, something that never could have happened a year before.

Also in May, several Quakers managed to obtain a pardon not only for their own believers in jails but other dissenters as well. John Bunyan was released from jail more than twelve years after his first arrest. And he was allowed to preach.

On Christmas Eve of 1672, John walked the high road out of Bedford and thought about his forty-four years here. Forty-four. Few men lived to be that old. That had to be God's blessing number one, but there were many others, too.

To be counted among the lesser blessings was the road itself. The Bedfordshire roads were a royal mess in spring and fall. Rain softened the mud so that wheels could cut the ruts deeper. The ruts filled with water for months at a time; not only was the mud itself slippery, but slick, greenish slime grew on the walls of the ruts and made them slipperier still. Ah, but winter—

This evening the road was frozen solid and beaten down flat. The ruts had leveled out and this country dirt was as firm as those fancy streets in London—and a far sight smoother than London cobbles. More than most men, John Bunyan, tinker, appreciated a firm, smooth road.

Major blessings included his family. Behind him walked John Junior and Thomas, both hefty boys, strong and lilting in their steps. Mary and little Liz were grown women now. And here beside him walked his own Elizabeth with six-year-old Sarah in hand and baby Joseph on her arm. Sarah bounded on ahead.

Elizabeth nudged his arm. "You have the happiest smile on your face for a man walking in such a cold and bitter wind."

He chuckled. "The wind is free, and so am I."

She poked a finger gently into his middle. "There's plenty of wind, and there's plenty of you, too. You've picked up a lot of weight since you got out of jail last May." She frowned. "I hope those days are over."

"I think they are." John watched the naked black branches of the oak trees rattle about in the unfettered wind. "When I applied for that license to preach they gave it to me. Brother Ruffhead made known the meeting place—his barn—and no one has raided it. When Josiah bought that

barn from Justice Crompton in Elstow, the justice
knew what we wanted it for and sold it anyway.
And when Josiah indentured the property to the
church members it was all recorded openly. No,
dear, I think England has grown up a little, and
our troubles are about over."

In the distance behind them the church bells
called vespers. Like little Sarah, they sang with
extra energy on Christmas Eve.

Here they were at last, at Josiah Ruffhead's
barn in the orchard. John stopped in mid-stride to
stare. The barn doors stood open; he could see
nothing but people in the torchlight inside. People
stood around the doors outside. More people waited among the trees in the orchard. And here came
still more people hurrying along the frozen roads
in the frozen wind and down the frozen lane.

Elizabeth gripped his arm the way a plowboy
hangs onto a hard-headed horse. She never had
liked crowds.

The brand new deacon, John Fenne, waved to
John and shouted from the barn doorway. The
great crowd quieted. John Fenne led the meeting
with a prayer and a hymn from the doorway. He
stepped aside and nodded toward John.

Brother Fenne's idea was as good as any. John
planted his huge body square in the doorway so
he could address both insiders and outsiders. His
voice could be loud enough to call hogs from a
mile off. He'd need that volume tonight, to be
heard by all in this wind.

"Brethren," he announced, "I've a few words
tonight about Jesus and His birth. But first I want

to introduce our deacon here, John Fenne, for many of you are strangers from outside the area. Take a bow, John."

Embarrassed, the quiet little man popped up and sat down hastily.

"Two years ago, we had to take our life in our hands—literally—to meet like this. Some were hanged, many were punished. Some suffered more than others. John here, and some others, were fined for what is legal to do today. John lost everything he had, trying to pay his fine. I trust all of you came prepared to make a gift toward the Lord's work. We'll take the offering right now. And keep in mind that what you give tonight is going to go to John Fenne and his family and the others who helped him. Two-and-a-half years ago he gave up everything he owned, and it's high time we helped restore a little."

John Fenne sat stunned; his mouth dropped open wide enough for a rabbit to jump in. He clamped it shut and shook his head wildly. *No, no, no!* his waving hands cried.

Yes, yes, yes! said John Bunyan's smug grin.

Sister Cooper started a hymn, since John Fenne seemed at a loss for words. John loved music, and he joined in the hymn as loudly as anyone else. So many voices sang! They sounded sweeter than church bells, for they were human voices praising God. Church bells, lovely as they sounded, were only chunks of metal who would not speak without a bell-ringer. They had no heart and mind with which to praise God on their own.

John looked at the crowd of faces singing. He

did not know most of them. There was Tom
Crocker, who came every week from Kimbolton
clear over in Huntington County. Many others, he
knew, came from afar.

These people should not have to come so far to
hear preaching. John decided suddenly that he
would begin a new project. He would help other
men become good preachers. And he would help
other groups of dissenters start up their own
meetings. That way the word of God could be
preached all over, and not just in Josiah Ruffhead's barn doorway. Yes! A good plan! John
would work out details and present it to the local
elders.

And now the voices like church bells had ended
their singing.

John Bunyan began to preach.

18

The Farmer in the Dell

March 4, 1675

"Brother Bunyan!"

Here came Sister Stubbes waddling down the flagstones from her front door to her gate. Little threads and wisps of gray hair sneaked out from under her ruffled dust cap. The lady herself bulged out over her tightly-tied apron strings and ballooned out below them. Her apron, once white, would never be white again; it was too blotched with the stains of a thousand delicious dinners.

John hauled his chunky bay horse to a stop beside the Stubbes's gate. "G'day, Sister Stubbes!"

She wiped her thick hands nervously on her apron. "Sam the brazier says the Act of Indulgence has been canceled. They can't do that, can they?"

She gripped her gate now with both hands, just a bit winded from that headlong dash of thirty feet.

"The act was a proclamation, not a true parliamentary act. The king can wipe it away just as easily as he proclaimed it."

"Oh, my! And he did so?"

"And he did so." John shifted in his saddle. "The king's latest proclamation says we must worship only in the state church; nor can we preach outside that church. Since February."

"Oh, my," she moaned. Her nervous hands clung to each other trembling. "Oh, my." Her watery eyes looked up at him. "You've been preaching a lot since February, and I've been coming to your meetings."

"Then I guess we must be outlaws, Sister Stubbes." John grinned and reached out with his own burly hand to her. "And I can't think of a Christian I'd rather be an outlaw with than you."

The chubby face widened suddenly into the brightest smile. Her hand buried itself in his, and she squeezed his fingers. "Oh, Brother Bunyan! You don't look the least bit frightened. I must study your example and take heart. It's not the end of the world, is it!"

"Hardly. In fact, it was unusual to be able to meet openly. This is the way our world usually is, and our Lord has kept us thus far."

"Yes." She gave his hand another squeeze and let go. "Thank you, Brother Bunyan, and God speed!"

"God bless us all, sister." John waved good-bye and thunked his heels in his horse's ribs. The bay gelding sighed and plodded out into the muddy road, on the way again.

Let's see. John took mental count. This was

March 4. Next week he was scheduled to preach in London town, and Wednesday a few days hence he was to preach in Stony Stratford. And then Friday a fortnight hence he would be—

His schedule was getting all confused. He was riding around preaching so much that he had no time any more for tinkering. Fortunately, both his sons had picked up the trade. As a matter of fact, Elizabeth was getting along quite well, for both John Junior and Thomas were contributing to the family finances. John himself drew some money preaching, and now and then he received a publication fee for a pamphlet or book.

John's chunky bay horse wound down the narrow road into a dark little dell. Naked tree branches arched almost completely over the road here. John could see the first tiny hints of leaf buds. His horse's feet made quiet splacking sounds in the mud.

From around the bend in the road came very noisy splacking sounds. Now here came Farmer Clemens riding through this dell on one of his horses. And what a horse!

There are lightweight horses and heavyweight horses. Lightweight horses are good for riding and for pulling carts in cities. Heavy horses are good only for war. A man and his armor together might weigh four hundred pounds. It takes a considerable horse to carry four hundred pounds very far.

But soldiers these days were not wearing armor much, for modern muskets could punch holes in just about any armor. Fewer and fewer great hors-

es were used in battle. Everyone in England
thought that huge horses were a thing of the past
—everyone except Farmer Clemens.

A century before, when King Henry VIII had
proclaimed that any horse less than five feet high
was to be destroyed (showed how much Henry
knew about good horses; about as much as
Charles Second knew about true worship), Farmer Clemens's grandfather began breeding horses
for size and strength. His grandson here was still
at it.

Farmer Clemens was riding one of his magnificent mares. Her chestnut hide glowed, even in this
dull spring overcast. Her legs were gateposts, her
neck a tree trunk. She was too broad-chested to fit
through a kitchen door. Her dark brown mane
and tail flowed like angel hair, and those wonderful silken tufts called feathers rippled around her
ankles. As Farmer Clemens came down through
the dell, John appreciated just how big this horse
was. She arched her neck and tucked her nose in
as her rider drew in the reins, and still her eye was
nearly level with John's.

John smiled. "Good to see you, Brother Clemens. What brings you out beyond Bedford
today?"

"The magistrates. They're waiting for you at
your house, John, with a warrant for your arrest.
Your wife's some upset."

"For preaching, no doubt."

"Mostly for failure to take Communion at St.
Cuthbert's, as I understand it. Something about

excommunicating you, too."

"Ah, well. Not the first time. I suppose I'd best go face it."

The old farmer studied him from his seat on high. "I hear you're supposed to preach in London next week."

"That's so."

"I hear, too, that the folks in London are so eager to hear your messages that they only need a day's notice that you're coming, and they fill the meeting hall."

"That's sometimes so," John replied modestly.

"And now you're gonna ride right into Bedford and let the magistrates cheat those poor London believers out of their chance to hear God's Word." The farmer's eyes, hard as steel, glared at John from under bushy brown brows.

"What do you suggest?"

The eyes softened the least bit. "There's more people who need you outside the jail than there are lice what need you inside the cell."

John chuckled. "Ah, but to the lice in the jail cell, I'm lifeblood."

"And y're lifeblood to us who needs God's Word. Go to London now. There's a hundred believers there who'll be happy to provide you a room. Charles Doe, the combmaker in Southwark—"

John shook his head. "I'm not a city man, George. I'm a country preacher. I don't mind going into the city for a day or two, but this is my home. Besides, that warrant would follow me and get someone in London into trouble."

"Well, ye better think of something soon. We're

coming close to Bedford and—uh oh!"

From the tanner's cottage on the edge of town, someone shouted. Two men appeared in the muddy road by an oak tree.

George Clemens dragged his vast horse to a halt. "Know 'em?"

"One of them. Old Bill Swinton has made a lifetime trade out of spying on dissenters and reporting to the churchmen. He even climbs trees to find out where we're meeting. And the fellow in the black greatcoat is the magistrate."

"On behalf of those good folks in London town—" Farmer Clemens reined his hulking mare aside suddenly, right into John's horse. The bay stumbled and lunged to avoid being squashed. "Down Rowe Lane!" the farmer shouted.

John dug his heels hard into the gelding's ribs. Thoroughly surprised, the old horse lurched into a clumsy run. The heavy mare beside him kept pace easily. All splashing and slipping, the horses galloped together down the rain-sodden lane. Here at the bottom of the dell a little creek crossed the path.

John's bay gelding shortened stride, gathered itself, and with a mighty heave flung itself across the muddy stream. John very nearly came unseated. He glanced back toward George.

The giant old mare never paused. Without breaking stride, as if the creek were only a tiny ribbon, she splashed across with feet the size of dinner plates.

"This way!" The farmer turned aside into Elder Rowe's hayfield. The mat of grass had been crushed and killed by winter snow, and the new spring green had not yet appeared. George drew his mare to a walk. The horses' feet squooshed in the rotten grass mat. Not even George's heavy horse left any marks in the spongy stuff.

George turned his mare presently, and they angled up toward a dense little woodlot. George was smiling. "Lotsa people claim the heavy horse ain't good for nothing, now they don't use 'em for war much anymore. Good for everything, I say. Go anywhere you want to go on one of these. Pull anything you want pulled. Better'n oxen for plowing and carting."

John just sniffed. "Doubt you'll go through that woodlot up ahead. The trees are too close. Too brushy."

"Eh." The steely eyes twinkled. "You just follow, Brother Bunyan." He urged his mare up into the wood edge with its heavy tangle of haw, berry bushes, and slender alders.

The friendly giant lowered her head a little and simply walked on. She walked on the bushes, she walked on the saplings. What her huge chest failed to shove aside her huge feet crushed. She crashed and snapped her way through the woods carelessly, effortlessly. John's gelding followed behind in her path of destruction.

The farmer did not stop until they had crossed the hill. They emerged from the woodlot, and John found himself near the road to Stony Stratford.

George stopped his wonderful horse and turned to John. "You go on to Stony Stratford and find someone's attic to live in for a couple weeks. I'll go back to Bedford and tell your good wife where you'll be. She can come to you with meals, and news, or whatever."

The steel eyes poured out concern. "People need what you offer, brother. They need to hear your preaching all the same as they need your writing. And I'll be diddled if we're gonna let those magistrates throw a kink in your plowline just because they feel like it. G'day, brother."

"G'day, George. Thank you." John would have said more, but already the farmer was hauling his massive mare around. With a fluid grace you would never expect in an animal so large, she wheeled and jogged off flatfooted toward Bedford town.

Now what? This business of hiding from the law was something new to John, and already he didn't like it. Was he doing the right thing or the wrong thing? He wished that God would send him some sort of a sign that he was indeed supposed to travel on to Stony Stratford.

His horse was tired. The first thing he must do was simply to sit right here a few minutes while the bay gelding rested.

Here came a man walking out from the direction of Stony Stratford. Should John Bunyan, brand new fugitive, hide? Or should he greet the fellow? He recognized the face but could not remember the name. This man was a member of the local congregation of dissenters in Stony Stratford.

The fellow raised his hand in greeting. "Why,

Brother Bunyan! Praise the Lord! Mightily pleased to see you. We'd heard there was a warrant issued for you this morning. We were afraid you would end up back in jail and couldn't come talk to us the way you'd planned."

John smiled. "Thanks to a friend with a giant horse, I'm still at large."

"Eh, that'll be George Clemens. Thinks his horse can do everything but walk on water. Sure is cranky on his great horses, ain't he?"

"With good reason. He feels I should come along into Stony Stratford now, though I'm not to preach there for a couple days yet."

"Good! Good! You can stay with the missus and me. Since our last daughter got married at Christmas, we've got the room. Let's go there now. My business will wait till tomorrow just fine."

John smiled and swung down off his weary horse. He walked beside the man and listened to all the news of the Stony Stratford meeting as they slopped along together down the road. So John had asked for a sign. My, but God was prompt! He chuckled to himself. Depend on the Lord for everything!

He prepareth the table before me in the presence of mine enemies.

I am the sheep of His pasture.

And so the sheep of God's pasture followed this godly shepherd's assistant to Stony Stratford and some hidden fold.

19

The Writer in the Prison Cell

April 1677

John laid his pen aside and pushed the paper away. He tilted his chair on two legs and leaned back against the stone prison wall. The sun, masked by a light April overcast, was past two o'clock. They would be speaking their vows now at the church altar. He waited with silence breathing in his ear.

In his imagination John could almost hear the shyly whispered "I do's." Suddenly the church bells exploded the silence and sent it flying. Like the morning stars, they sang for joy. Ah, sweet wedding bells—just listen to them! John's heart tickled with happiness, and his eyes got wet.

Elizabeth his daughter, the second child of his dear lost Mary, was now a married woman. Her bridegroom would sweep her away to a new life. She no longer belonged to John. She was another man's now.

John regretted very much all those years in

prison, for he could not watch Elizabeth and the others grow up. He could not often offer advice or share their joys and sorrows. He could not simply have a good time with them, as he so loved to do. He had missed many things a father does. It was a heavy burden for a man who enjoyed children.

The bells quieted eventually, reluctantly. The silence returned on tiptoe and paused again beside him.

"Papa?" Elizabeth's soft voice came from the cell door. John jumped to his feet so quickly he almost tipped over his table. He pressed against the cell door.

Elizabeth's pale hand slipped between the bars. "We're leaving now, Papa. I had to stop by to tell you it was a happy wedding, but it would have been happier if you were there. I love you, Papa."

"And I love you. God bless you, honey."

Her cool little hand grasped his great thick one, and then she was gone.

Very sad even as he was very happy, John wandered back to his chair and table and sat down. He picked up his pen again, but no words came.

"Visitor, Johnny," the jailer called. Might it be a wedding guest come to offer congratulations to the father of the bride? John doubted it. The door creaked open, and in came Nathaniel Ponder.

Publisher Ponder was a weighty fellow indeed, if you looked at his waistline. To keep his balance with such a bulky tummy, he walked with something of a backwards tilt. This tucked his many chins all in close to his chest and thrust the ample belly even further out. He came waddling in, his toes pointing outward, his boots headed in slightly different directions than the man himself.

"Ah, John! Glad to see you, but sorry to see you so. You've been in jail what—four months now?"

"This time. Aye, since late last year. How's publishing?"

The hefty gentleman stirred a wad of straw beside John and carefully settled himself onto it, like a cautious hen upon a nest. "Good. Very good. Hear your works are selling well, too. These jail terms now and then don't seem to stop you from spreading the Word."

"They don't help it much, though—don't help my home life much, either."

Mr. Ponder grunted. "Saw *The Strait Gate* on the shelf in a London newsagent's a fortnight ago. Came out last year, didn't it? Seventy-six?"

John nodded.

"And that light in the darkness treatise—?

"*Light for Them That Sit in Darkness*. Two years ago. Wrote that one in jail also. That little jail on the Swan Bridge."

"You were warranted in seventy-five, too?"

John nodded. "A friend warned me, and I went into hiding for a month or so. Had these sermons scheduled, you see. But we have spies in the shire, and the magistrates didn't have too much trouble finding me once I came back from London. Hiding doesn't do much good."

"Writing anything now? I'm looking for good material."

John smiled and leaned back in his chair. "It happens I am. Something a little different from the usual messages I've written."

"Not too different, I hope. You'll never do better, you know, than you did with *Grace Abounding*. I know you wrote it twenty-two years ago, but it's still selling well."

John smiled. Should he mention that Mr. Ponder here had paid him only a very small fee for that work? Or that Mr. Ponder here was pocketing all the profits since then? He skipped that point and said instead, "I'm writing an allegory. A man named Christian falls into a deep sleep and dreams about a journey from the City of Destruction to the Celestial City. It will show the walk every pilgrim of the faith must make to reach eternal life."

The publisher wagged his ample head. "It won't sell. Allegory's old stuff. Nobody wants it. Stick to your sermons and treatises. That's where you'll make your mark!"

"I don't care about making my mark. I'm not looking for fame. I want to show people how to find eternal life, and an allegory is something every common man can understand. The people this Christian meets will be named after their faults or virtues, and they will show the faults and virtues in their actions. I want to call it *Pilgrim's Progress*."

"Nice title," the publisher admitted. "Catchy."

"The burden of sin," John continued, "will be pictured by a huge, heavy bundle on Christian's back."

"A bundle! No explanation for it? Just this mysterious burden?"

John smiled sadly. "I know a thing or two about burdens, Brother Ponder."

"Yes." The publisher grew quiet. "Yes, you do. All kinds of burdens. You're in here on a church offense, I take it."

"As always. Yes."

The publisher nodded. He began the slow job of getting his bulk back onto his feet. "Know a Robert Blaney? Or a Thomas Kelsey?"

"Both. Good solid Christian men. Londoners."

Brother Ponder now had both feet under him. He stood upright. He stretched. "Don't see how you can stand it in here." He brushed himself off. "They're going to put up bond for you. Sign papers to get you out, they say."

"They don't expect me to give up preaching, I hope."

"Why can't you just tinker, like every other tinker?"

John shrugged and smiled. "No forge. I gave my forge and anvil to my son John. He has the whole business now, and doing very nicely with it, I might add. Leaves me completely free to ride around and serve the Lord full-time."

Brother Ponder snorted. "Tell you what. You want your allegory published? I doubt it will do anything, but I'll publish it. Pay you a flat fee. None of this part-of-every sale stuff; you wouldn't make as much that way as the fee will bring in. When will it be ready?"

"December. January."

The portly man nodded. "I'm doing you a favor, John. Trust me. It won't sell."

"Do you suppose," John asked, "that it is neither you nor I who controls sales, but God? If God doesn't like it, it will wither and fade. If He decides to use it for His work, it will sell well. I only write the work. God uses it."

"Nice theology, but I know publishing. God bless you, John." The man left, and John settled back at his writing table.

In his mind, he was imagining what that horrible monster Apollyon might look like to Christian.

20

The Guest in Southwark

August 1688

This was supposed to be the middle of August! It felt near freezing. Icy wind had no trouble biting through John's light cape. He had left home dressed for summer, and here was the weather trying to pretend it was winter.

He rode through the streets of Reading town, rigid on his horse. The tighter he kept his muscles, the warmer he stayed.

A young man waved cheerfully from a bakery door. John knew him as one of the members of the local church here in Reading. The lad could well be cheerful; that bakery oven right behind him kept him toasty warm.

"Bishop Bunyan!" There was Sister Hawkes calling him "bishop" again. True, he had started a lot of churches all around southern England. True, he rode from place to place almost constantly, helping his little congregations, solving quarrels, smoothing things out. It was why he was in

Reading today. True, his preaching was very popular; he filled every meetinghouse he preached in. True, these were all jobs a bishop might be expected to do. Still he wished they wouldn't stick that bishop title onto him. He was a brother. That was all. A brother in Christ.

He got off his horse beside Sister Hawkes, and his feet ached when they touched the ground. He tucked his big Bible under his arm.

"What a hideous day," the lady moaned. "Something you'd expect of November, not August. They're waiting for you, the old goat and his snip of a son both."

"Now, now, sister. Be charitable."

They walked together to a little cottage behind the river road. Sister Hawkes explained to him the problem of a man and his son, and how angry the two men were with each other. John had settled more than a few family squabbles of this sort.

The cottage door was closed tight against the unseasonal cold. John pushed it open and stepped inside.

"Ah! Here's Bishop Bunyan!" Elder James hopped to his feet.

The fireplace was full of hot, cheerful flames. John hurried right to it, and someone gave him a chair. On one side of him sat a grumpy old man with a long, hooked nose. On his other sat a grumpy young man with a long, hooked nose. Two other elders besides Brother James stood behind the chairs.

Elder James was apologizing for having to ask John to come this far distance. And now they were hushed, watching him, waiting.

John held his hands out to the fire and rubbed them. Ah, warmth! He looked from man to man at the two beside him. "So, gentlemen. I trust each of you has in mind what you will tell me—how you will present your side of this argument."

Both men opened their mouths, and John quickly raised his hand. Both mouths closed.

"Before we begin that, open your Bibles, please."

"Left mine home," the father muttered. "Sorry, Brother Bunyan."

"I don't own one yet," the son admitted. "No money to buy one."

"I'm sure then we'll all fit around mine." John opened his Bible to Ephesians, chapter six, and plopped the big book on the son's lap. "Verses one through three, please."

The young man looked at him a moment. The lad was probably not yet twenty, but he read very well. "Children, obey your parents in the Lord; for this is right. Honour thy father and mother; which is the first commandment with promise: That it may be well with thee, and thou mayest live long on the earth."

John pulled his Bible back onto his lap and gave it to the father. "Verse four, please. Also nine. It pertains indirectly. And ten, too."

The father's rumbly voice droned. " 'And, ye fathers, provoke not your children to wrath; but bring them up in the nurture and admonition of the Lord.' Uh, 'And, ye masters—' "

"You are, in a sense, a master."

"And, ye masters, do the same things unto them, forbearing threatening; knowing that your Master also is in heaven; neither is there any respect of persons with Him. Finally, my brethren, be strong in the Lord, and in the power of His might.'"

John dragged his Bible back onto his own lap. He was getting a headache for some reason. "You have just read God's will for you. You don't need me to tell you whether you have fallen short. Young man, as you know I spent over twelve years in jail altogether. My wife raised our children. I know more than most men do how precious children are, because I could not be with mine. You are very precious to your father. And when you hurt him, his pain is far more than if some stranger hurt him. You must be very kind to fathers and mothers. You can hurt them so easily."

John turned to the father. "You did not stop being his father when he grew up. When he looks at you he sees his father and also the heavenly Father. You are the example of a father, all fathers —what you want him to be when he is a father. Are you careful to be the best example you can be?"

John closed his Bible. "I suppose I could hear both sides of your fight and make some sort of decision. But how much better it would be if you treated each other gently and worked out your problems together. Each side give a little. You owe each other the best because you are father and son. I must preach near Whitechapel in London in a few days. Then I will return, Lord willing, through Reading here. If you have solved your problem I will rejoice with you. If you have not, I will help you work on it together. You the precious child and you the example of all fathers. Can you do it?"

"We will do it," said the son with conviction. The father mumbled something.

John stood up, and his ears rang. He blessed everyone, spoke a prayer, and left the warm little cottage, back into the biting wind.

Obviously Sister Hawkes had been listening closely at the door. She pressed in beside him as he walked to his horse. "How wise of you, Bishop Bunyan! They're good fellows, really, both of them."

"Oh?" I hear they are a goat and a snip." He hauled himself wearily into his saddle.

Her whole face turned red to match her ears. "Brother Bunyan!" She bit her lip. "I apologize. I will be more careful what I say."

"Good. We're called to account for every word, you know, and I hate to see you get into trouble. God bless you, Sister Hawkes." John dragged his horse's head around and turned it east along the river road.

A cold chill rippled down his spine and raised goose bumps on his arms and legs. God made weather, of course, but John assumed He used natural forces to make it with. But then, what natural forces could bring snowflakes out of the August sky? Mid summer! Here they came, big fluffy white blobs. The swirling little fluffies became cold, hard, stinging ice-flakes. Pelting rain joined the painful snow. Within the hour, John was soaked to the skin.

He entered London town the next day. To one who grew up near the little bridge in Bedford across the River Ouse, London Bridge was a marvel. The only link between the city on the north bank of the Thames and the sprawling new growth on the south bank (which included several theaters and those horrible bear-baiting arenas), London Bridge was wide enough to let traffic flow in both directions at once. But it was much wider than that. Shops lined both sides of the bridge all the way across the river. Above the shops were rooms where the merchants lived. These apartments came together in the middle of the bridge, forming a great tunnel between the city and Southwark.

But then, the whole huge city was a marvel to a country boy.

It was nearly dark. Almost all the shops were shuttered. Wet and shivering, John rode through the narrow streets. He knew the city well now, for he often preached in London. His tired horse stumbled up the slope of Snow's Hill.

Here was the little grocery shop he was looking for. He climbed down stiffly and pounded on the door. His horse shook itself. Yellow candlelight promised warmth as it leaked out a crack in the shutters upstairs.

"Bishop Bunyan?" John Strudwick's voice called, warm and welcome, from overhead.

"Indeed, sir, and God bless!"

Ah. In a moment John would be safe and cozy among friends. He would be able to rest and get rid of this chill. While waiting for Brother Strudwick, John might as well unsaddle. He picked at the little buckles on his horses girth, but his fingers were too cold and numb to open them. His toes burned; his body shook.

A small girl with huge dark eyes opened the door for him. "Uncle John says to leave the horse and he'll take care of it. Come up, he says."

"Thank you." John followed the child's candle through the black grocery shop to the rear stairs. He climbed the stairs halfway and stopped.

"Let us rest a moment. It's been a long day." He plunked down on the wooden steps. The child sat down beside him.

She looked at him with her head tilted. "Papa says you are a great and famous man, but you look too friendly to be important."

John laughed. "Ah, yes, I'm important. You see, Jesus died for me, and that makes me very important. Know who else is important?"

The head wagged no, and those eyes were pools of rich warmth.

"You are. You're just as important as I am, because Jesus died for you, too."

The pools grew bigger. "Me?" she breathed.

"You." John leaned back and tried to get comfortable. You can't be comfortable sitting in a narrow staircase—not when you're as big and bulky as John Bunyan. "Almost exactly two years ago—in 'eighty-six—I wrote my favorite book."

"*Pilgrim's Progress*? Papa says that's England's favorite book. Ever so many people have read it."

"That was one of my favorites. My very favorite is a little book called *Country Rimes, A Book for Boys and Girls*. It's also called *Country Rimes for Children*."

"Poetry?"

John nodded. "I grew up in a little farming village, and I like to talk about country people and farm things. Lots of that in the book. And I made up some little poems to tell children like you about God's love. It was such fun to do. And children seem to like it."

"I'd like it."

"I'll see that you get a copy." John lurched to his feet and swayed a bit. "Now, let's go on up and greet your uncle John. I'm ready to eat and rest."

She bounded to her feet. Her small, cool hand gripped his. And together they climbed the stairs.

One would think that a day of quiet rest and good food would make a new man out of tired John Bunyan. It did not. He felt worse than ever when he set out for Whitechapel. Chills and hot flashes took turns making him miserable. His lungs hurt every time he took a deep breath. He had to take lots of deep breaths, too, for he would preach in a large hall and had to be heard from end to end of it.

He knew the hall was Mr. Gammon's meeting-house on Boar's Head Yard. He knew it was somewhere off Petticoat Lane in Whitechapel. But he had trouble remembering how to get there and needed John Strudwick's help to find it.

He needed no help remembering his message. The text was John 1:13, a verse he loved. After preaching, he would rest a few more days at the grocer's before he went back to Reading and then home. He did not look forward to that long hard road to Reading. After all, he was about three months short of his sixtieth birthday. He was getting to be an old man, and he must learn to take life a little slower.

Two more days of rest at Strudwick's, however, did not help his illness at all. The fever got worse. Lying on his sickbed, John had plenty of time to think. He thought about his next treatise, but he didn't feel like writing anything down. Not just then. Later.

Days and nights melted into each other, and he lost track of them. He wished Elizabeth were here. Sarah had married two years ago, which left only little Joseph at home. Joseph was old enough to travel well. Perhaps Elizabeth could come down here. He asked, and he could not remember what John Strudwick's good wife said in reply. He asked about his dear blind Mary, too. They had to remind him that Mary had died several years ago.

Those things should not be slipping his mind like that. It must be the fever.

One of the nicest things about London was all the churches. The huge St. Paul's Cathedral, whose steeple John could see from Bedford on clear days, had burned in the great London fire of 1666. But there were many others with marvelous bell towers. Indeed, London was a city full of bells, and John had always loved bells.

Also, because London was full of people—four hundred thousand of them!—there were always weddings and funerals and other occasions for the bells to sing about. You could here bells often and at almost any time of day.

John lay in the rooms above the grocery store with the window open and listened to the bells.

They reminded him of his sister Margaret, gone so many years, and his natural mother. Was his lively, lusty father in heaven? He did not know. He knew for certain his first wife, Mary, was. So was blind Mary.

On August 31, 1688, John was allowed to join them.

The bells sang just for him.

Dates in John Bunyan's Life

1199	William Bunion recorded in Bedford/Elstow area
1623, January 10	Thomas Bunyan marries Ann Pinney
1627	Ann dies early in the year
1627, May 23	Thomas marries Margaret Bentley
1628, November	John Bunyan christened (the Church of England christened newborns; this was probably John's birth month)
1630, March 7	Margaret the sister born
1633, December 1	William the brother born
1641	Grandfather Thomas dies, leaving John sixpence in his will
1644, June	John's mother, Margaret, dies
1644, July	Sister Margaret dies
1644, August	Father, Thomas, remarries
1644, November	John enters the army at age sixteen
1647, June or July	John musters out of the army, takes up tinkering

1648	John marries at age twenty
1650, early	Daughter Mary is born blind
1650, late	Daughter Elizabeth is born
1654-1658	Sons John, Jr., and Thomas are born
1658	Oliver Cromwell, who encouraged people to worship outside the state church, dies
1659	John's wife dies, he marries again—Elizabeth
1660, November 12	John is arrested and spends seven weeks in prison
1661, January	John tried by Justice Kelynge, sentenced to three months' imprisonment, then deportation
1661, April 23	Charles II crowned king of England; John's deportation is postponed so he can apply for amnesty along with others
1662	Act of Conformity makes it illegal to worship anywhere but in the state church; John was sentenced under a much older act
1665-1666	The Great Plague strikes England, especially London
1666	John's autobiography, *Grace Abounding to the Chief of Sinners*, is published, becomes very popular
1666	John is released from prison awhile, is rearrested
1666, late	Daughter Sarah is born
1666, September 2	The Great Fire of London destroys three-fifths of the city,

	including St. Paul's Cathedral and eighty-eight other churches
1670, May 15	John Fenne and others are severely persecuted while John is in jail
1671	Persecution eases; John is elected pastor of the Bedford meeting, applies for a license to preach
1672	Act of Indulgence, a proclamation by the king, permits some worship outside the state church
1672, May 9	John gets his license to preach
1672, May 17	Released officially from jail, one of the six religious dissenters in Bedford covered by a Quaker pardon
1672, August	Josiah Ruffhead's barn and orchard become the official meeting place—and remained so for centuries
1672	Son Joseph born
1673	Son Thomas put on church roll at about age seventeen
1675, February 3	Another proclamation cancels the Act of Indulgence
1675, March 4	John is warranted for arrest, goes into hiding a month, spends six months in jail
1676, late	Arrested again
1677, April	Daughter Elizabeth marries
1677, June	John is released on bond, is probably free five or six months

1677	Son John takes over his tinkering full-time
1677, December 22	*Pilgrim's Progress* licensed and registered
1678, February 18	Publishes *Pilgrim's Progress*; the book is a huge success
1680	Publishes *Life and Death of Mr. Badman* to show the opposite of Christian's life in *Pilgrim's Progress*
1682	*The Holy War* published
1684	The second part of *Pilgrim's Progress* appears, in which a woman, Christiana, makes the journey to eternal life
1685, February	Charles II dies; James II becomes king
1685	John sees severe persecution ahead with the change in government and has his will made; it will be found in its hiding place two hundred years after he dies
1686	His daughter Sarah marries
1686	*Country Rimes for Boys and Girls*, his children's poetry book, appears
1688, January	Persecution eases and dissenters are actually elected to the Bedford Council
1688, August 19	John comes to London to preach at Whitechapel
1688, August 21	His illness worsens
1688, August 31	John Bunyan dies in London and is buried there
1688, September 4	Bedford meeting learns of his death

1688, September 18	Bedford meeting elects Ebenezer Chandler to replace Bishop Bunyan; Chadler will serve 57 years
1691	Wife Elizabeth dies
Today	More than three hundred years later, *Pilgrim's Progress* appears in nearly one hundred languages, showing people all over the world the way to eternal life.

Moody Press, a ministry of the Moody Bible Institute, is designed for education, evangelization, and edification. If we may assist you in knowing more about Christ and the Christian life, please write us without obligation: Moody Press, c/o MLM, Chicago, Illinois 60610.